SHARING THE DARKNESS

SHARING THE DARKNESS

The Spirituality of Caring

SHEILA CASSIDY

Foreword by Jean Vanier

ORBIS BOOKS

Maryknoll, New York 10545

The Catholic Foreign Mission Society of America (Maryknoll) recruits and trains people for overseas missionary service. Through Orbis Books, Maryknoll aims to foster the international dialogue that is essential to mission. The books published, however, reflect the opinions of their authors and are not meant to represent the official position of the society.

Copyright © 1991 by Sheila Cassidy
Published by Orbis Books, Maryknoll, NY 10545
Originally published in Great Britain in 1988 by Darton, Longman and Todd Ltd., 89 Lillie Road, London SW6 1UD. The present edition has been slightly revised.

Manufactured in the United States of America

Thanks are due to the following for permission to quote copyright material: Cairns Publications, from *Healing More or Less* and *Prayer at Night* by the Rev. James E. Cotter; Harper & Row Inc, from *Holy the Firm* by Annie Dillard; David Higham Associates Ltd, from *Our World* by John Harriott; SCM Press Ltd, from *Christian Neurosis* by Pierre Solignac; Stainer & Bell Ltd, from "Mother Teresa" in *The Two Way Clock* by Sydney Carter. Author and publisher would be glad to hear from any copyright holder whom they have been unable to trace, so that they can make acknowledgement in future editions of this book.

Library of Congress Cataloging-in-Publication Data

Cassidy, Sheila, 1937-
    Sharing the darkness : the spirituality of caring / Sheila Cassidy ; foreword by Jean Vanier.
        p. cm.
    ISBN 0-88344-779-7 (pbk.)
    1. Hospice care. I. Title.
R726.8.C42 1991
259'.4 – dc20   91-28462
                                                       CIP

For my teachers

George Pickering
who taught me to be a doctor

Michael Hollings
who taught me how to pray

Jim Drewery
who taught me how to survive

There is however a quantum leap from preparing a lecture to writing a book, a fact of literary life which I was to learn the hard way over the coming year. I say this by way of explanation, for the circumstances in which the book was written have had a major influence upon its shape and character. The greatest problem turned out to be that of continuity, for working full time as I do, all my writing has to be done in trains or on weekends. That which is unfinished by Sunday night must lie fallow until the next free weekend, with the result that both the flow of ideas and the mood in which they were written are difficult to recapture.

Another problem was that the book took a quite unexpected change of direction half-way through: what had started life as an exploration of the spirituality of the care of the dying, broadened to encompass all those involved in professions or ministries of caring—perhaps even all Christians. The change happened the Easter which I spent at L'Arche community at Trosly Breuil outside Paris. It was there, as an outsider to the community, that I saw more clearly than ever before the prophetic nature of caring for those who are, in economic terms, useless. It is a lavishing of precious resources, our precious ointment on the handicapped, the insane, the rejected and the dying that most clearly reveals the love of Christ in our times. It is this gratuitous caring, this unilateral declaration of love which proclaims the gospel more powerfully than bishops and theologians. It is an ongoing reenactment of the drama at the house at Bethany, when Mary took the alabaster box of ointment, of "Spikenard very precious," and poured it over Jesus' head. I wonder sometimes if either Mary or Jesus was aware of the full significance of this outrageous public gesture of love. Perhaps, like today's carers, they acted instinctively from their true centers, recognizing a need and moving out to meet it, whatever the price, whatever the consequences.

This book then is about the meaning and the cost of caring. It does not pretend to be either scholarly or exhaustive, but is rather an exploration, a series of reflections from the inside, from the eye of the storm. Because my own experience is with the sick and the dying, most of the illustrations are from this field, but I believe the ideas generated and the lessons learned

Introduction

IN SEARCH OF A SPIRITUALITY

This book, like many children born to impulsive, disorganized women, was conceived by accident and reared amid chaos. The first seeds were sown in 1985 when I was invited to speak on the rather ambiguous subject of "The Spirituality of the Carer." It took me a long time to work out what the title meant but I decided eventually that it must mean the spiritual stance of the carer and I set out to work out just what that stance should be. The first idea that came to me was the image of the carer as midwife: assisting at the birth of a dying person into a new life. Another line of thought was that it should be a paschal spirituality, a vision which encompassed both death and resurrection. Eventually, however, I fell back on my favorite quotation from the prophet Micah:

> This is what Yahweh asks of you, only this:
> That you act justly,
> love tenderly and walk humbly
> with your God.
>
> (Mic. 6:8)

The "act justly" I saw as an obligation to be professionally competent, the "love tenderly" a call to compassion, and the "walk humbly" a bowing down before God and the mystery of suffering. Thus equipped with a framework, I developed my theme and the lecture was duly delivered.

ACKNOWLEDGEMENTS

I am deeply grateful to the many people who have helped me bring this work to life; who have inspired, encouraged or provoked me to thought. I am especially indebted to the men and women of St. Luke's Hospice in Plymouth and the L'Arche Community at Trosly Breuil in France who more than anyone have revealed to me the prophetic message of unconditional loving. My special thanks are due to Angela Tilby whose gentle wisdom was crucial in the final shaping of the material and to Christine Sumner and Stephen James who labored so many hours over the manuscript. Lastly, my heart goes out to my patients, past, present and to come, for it is they who are the warp and the woof of my every day and therefore of this book.

S.C.

journey in and to the beatitudes. Sheila finds her strength in the good news of the gospels. But she reveals herself through this book not as someone very, very special, but rather as someone quite ordinary, but knowing she is loved by her God. Isn't that the ultimate secret of the gospels?, that we are all ordinary, born in littleness and called to die in littleness. But we are loved and have a mission to love. To pour that spikenard ointment, so precious and so costly, upon the feet of Jesus soon to die, is the same as pouring oneself out upon those who will die tomorrow and who today are apparently useless.

Perhaps the secret Sheila is revealing to us, the secret she has learned through her daily life and her life of prayer, is that the poor and the weak are not just objects of charity and love, even less are they useless and to be discarded or seen as a problem and a burden; but rather they are called to be a source of life for us all. If we come close to them, in some mysterious way they bring us to what is essential; they call us to truth, to competence, to compassion, and to centeredness.

This is truly a precious book, important not just for people in the hospice movement or in L'Arche, but for all those who are in the caring profession, and for all of us who are called to care for one another.

JEAN VANIER
L'Arche

is a link between the brokenness of people with a mental handicap and that of the assistants in L'Arche. That may seem to be a strange remark, possibly a bit impertinent or out of place. Don't you have to be very holy, wise and wholesome in order to be close to dying people or to people with a mental handicap? Don't you have to be very special and wonderful to be able to be close to dirty, "useless" and smelly people? I suppose that is the way most people would see assistants in L'Arche or the staff in the hospices for the dying. Strangely enough, it is not like that. To be close to people with handicaps, to live with them and enjoy their company, you have to be in contact with your own handicaps, learning to live with them and, I even dare to say, to enjoy their company. So it is for Sheila as she listens to people in pain, who are dying; she has to be able to listen to all that is painful, and to all that is dying within her own being. Can we truly be compassionate to others if we do not know how to be compassionate to ourselves?

What we are living in our L'Arche communities is similar in so many ways to what Sheila and others are living in the hospice movement. I suppose that is why I feel deeply in communion with her and with her vision of love and caring.

I find this book very beautiful because it is about people in their utter poverty, littleness, and vulnerability; not about those who pretend to be big and strong, who are successful and winning prizes, but who are also hiding their fears and vulnerability behind masks. This book is about people who are very earthy and very vulnerable; people who no longer wear masks because they do not even have the energy to maintain them. It is also about the people who truly care about those who have become vulnerable and who are dying. These carers are experiencing their own deepest fears. They themselves have become very vulnerable. They too no longer hide behind masks, masks of medical technique or of well-set formulas. So often they feel empty-handed and powerless. They let themselves be touched and their hearts be opened. Not only are they competent, which all doctors and nurses must be, but they are also compassionate.

Clearly, Sheila is walking with Jesus. From the prison he led her to the monastery; from the monastery, he led her to those who are dying. Her journey is a simple, beautiful one; it is the

FOREWORD

I first heard of Sheila Cassidy when I read her book *Audacity to Believe* telling the story of her life in Chile where she had gone to work as a doctor. She tells of her work amongst the very poor. One day friends asked her to treat a man with a bullet wound, a wounded revolutionary in hiding from the secret police. This was an unforgivable act in the eyes of the military and for that reason she was imprisoned and tortured. I was deeply touched as I read of her faith and courage, in the face of terrible fears and pain.

When I put the book down, renewed in inner peace, I knew that one day I would meet the woman who had written it.

We corresponded, and then one day we did meet: she came to spend a few days here in the community of L'Arche in Trosly, not far from Compiegne, in France. There I did not read her, but I listened to her. It was clear that since the end of *Audacity to Believe,* she had evolved and grown.

In 1978, Sheila abandoned medicine to enter a contemplative monastery. After the prison, it seemed necessary for her to enter another prison, opened now to prayer and to the heavens. But that was not her final path. Jesus is an incredible teacher. He has led her to greater earthiness, ordinariness and littleness. She then became the Medical Director responsible for a ten-bed hospice for the terminally ill in Plymouth, England.

This book is the story of her journey in the hospice. It is about people who are dying; it is about caring and love. It is also about her own personal journey; the way God is leading her through her own brokenness.

As I listen to Sheila when she comes to L'Arche, and as I read this book, I sense a deep link between her brokenness and the brokenness of the dying people she cares for; just as there

Contents

may be of relevance to a much wider audience, indeed to all those who find themselves drawn, for whatever reason, to accompany those in pain. The title *Sharing the Darkness* comes from the widow of Anglican writer J. B. Phillips, who, in telling of her husband's severe depression, wrote, "Jack found himself sharing the darkness with Michael Hollings," and "in the dark experience of his pain he could only repeat Michael's words: 'There is no way out, only a way forward.' "

What then is the essence of this book; for whom is it written? If I am truthful I suppose it was written for myself, because there were things that I wanted to say, ideas I wanted to explore. More than anything it arises from a deep conviction that we are all called to be holy, to love the Lord our God with heart, mind, and spirit and our neighbors as ourselves. For most of us, this call to holiness must be lived out right where we are, inserted in the midst of twentieth-century society. This is not a book for those who feel called to flee from a world they perceive to be wicked but for those of us whose vocation it is to discover the innate goodness in ordinary people, the face of Christ in all men and women. I believe that those who work with the handicapped, the dispossessed, and the dying have very expensive ringside seats at the fight: we have a close-up view of players who are stripped of sophistication and pretence, of the comforting outer garments with which people cover their nakedness, their vulnerability, and their shame. Surely then, we have a duty to report back the truth of what we see: that the facts are friendly; that the blind see, the lame walk, the lepers are cleansed, and the good news is proclaimed to the poor — that the kingdom of God is among us, and that herein lies our hope.

And if it should happen that you who pick up this book are sick or even dying, I hope you will find yourself at peace with what I write, for it comes not from book learning but from my own experience of caring and being cared for. More than anything I have discovered that the world is not divided into the sick and those who care for them, but that we are all wounded and that we all contain within our hearts that love which is for the healing of the nations. What we lack is the courage to start giving it away.

⊰{ 1 }⊱

CUT FROM THE LOOM

I said: In the noon of my life
I have to depart
for the gates of Sheol,
I am deprived of the rest of my years ...
My tent is pulled up, and thrown away
like the tent of a shepherd;
like a weaver you roll up my life
to cut it from the loom.
　　　　　from the canticle of Hezekiah
　　　　　　　　Isa. 38:10, 12

In seeking a spirituality for those who care for the dying, the first questions that must be asked are "Who are the people cared for? What are they like? What characterizes them, marks them out from their fellows?" The dying, and here I include anyone with an incurable illness, are essentially people on a journey. They are an uprooted people, dispossessed, marginalized, traveling fearfully into the unknown. The conditions and speed of the journey may vary—sometimes the movement is barely perceptible, like the moving sidewalks at the airport—but sometimes the trucks hurtle through the night, throwing their bewildered occupants from side to side with all the terror of the line to Auschwitz. Above all, the dying are alone and they are afraid.

Paradoxically these fears are rarely articulated, so strong is the cult of the stiff upper lip or the desire to protect those closest to them. The poems of the sixteen-year-old Indian girl Gitanjali, found after her death from cancer, give us a glimpse into this lonely hidden world of the dying:

> Tonight, as on other nights
> I'm walking alone
> Through the valley of fear.
> O God, I pray
> that you will hear me
> for only you alone know
> what is in my heart.
> Lift me out of this valley of despair
> and set my soul free.
>
> Gitanjali
> from *I'm Walking Alone*

What they want more than anything is that this thing should not be happening to them, that it should turn out to be a bad dream, that they should be rescued, cured, kissed better, made whole. But since this cannot be, they want someone to comfort them, to hold their hand, to face the unknown with them. They need a companion, a friend.

So the spirituality of those who care for the dying must be the spirituality of the companion, of the friend who walks alongside, helping, sharing and sometimes just sitting, empty-handed, when he would rather run away. It is a spirituality of *presence,* of being alongside, watchful, available; of being *there.*

It is interesting in this context to explore the meaning of the word *companion,* for it gives us a deeper insight, not only into the role but also the experience of the carer. The companion is one who shares bread; and the dying complain like the psalmist:

> The bread I eat is ashes
> My drink is mingled with tears.
> Ps. 102:9 (Grail)

Whoever would be a companion to the dying, therefore, must enter into their darkness, go with them at least part way along their lonely and frightening road. This is the meaning of *compassion:* to enter *into* the suffering of another, to share in some small way in their pain, confusion, and desolation.

Put like this, the care for the dying seems an impossibly daunting task. Who but a fool or a saint would deliberately expose themselves, day after day, to intolerable pain and sadness? And yet of course people do. Why? Who knows. I suppose the obvious answer is that it is a calling, what in religious jargon is called a vocation. Some people are attracted to this kind of work, they find they have a gift for it and discover that it is enormously rewarding. It is not easy — never that, but somehow what one pays out is given back a hundredfold.

What sort of people find themselves called to accompany the dying? At the psychological level one needs three basic attributes: the first is an intensely down-to-earth practicality that does not flinch from the impact of the disintegration of human bodies and minds; the second — and I believe it to be equally important — is an oversized sense of humor, for life and death is a terrible tragicomedy and as the saying goes, "If you didn't laugh, you'd have to cry." The third quality is a very special sort of sensitivity: a vulnerability to the pain of others that is often, but not always, the result of personal experience of suffering.

At a religious level perhaps the most important gift is a sort of paschal overview — the ability to hold *in the same focus* the harsh reality of suffering and the mind-boggling truth of resurrection, of life after death. One must develop the ability to stand with feet firmly planted on an earth inhabited by wounds and vomit bowls, but with the gaze focused beyond the mess of the here and now to a future of hope beyond imaginings. More than anything, one must know deep in one's guts that death is the beginning, not the end.

Arising from this concept of death as birth is the image of the carer as midwife. If death is in reality birth into new life, then the carer is one who attends the person in labor, comforting, encouraging, facilitating as new life emerges from the old. Watching people grow in spiritual stature is one of the most exciting aspects of working with the dying — as indeed it is in any ministry. Growth, however, is always the work of the spirit — one cannot make it happen; just try to provide an environment in which it can occur if it is meant to. And occur it does: people who seem quite ordinary gradually transcend their human bonds of fear and self-interest, until their only concern is for others. They become somehow translucent, incandescent, glowing like candles in the dark.

As I write today I think of three patients at present in the hospice: there is Arthur, the elderly cockney tugboat man from Gravesend who worries that his wife has made a terrible mistake in uprooting herself from London. He is sad that he is dying and he hates it when his leg hurts — but his real concern is for her. Then there is Margaret in her fifties, paralyzed from the waist down by the cancer in her spine, and worrying, not about herself but that Gordon, her husband, will not cope without her. And lastly, of course, there is Andrew, a bright thirteen-year-old, concerned above all to be the man about the house for his divorced mother and busily painting pictures which he sells to raise money for our building appeal. These are just three people we are caring for at the moment. I could think of so many more. Oddly enough it is the selfish ones who are uncommon and always take us by surprise.

From time to time I am asked if my contact with so much suffering makes me doubt the existence of God. Perhaps it should — but I can only grin and try to explain that, paradoxically, this work has given me an ever-deeper conviction of the existence of an all-powerful, all-loving God who has the whole world in his hands.

This conviction, I know, is shared by many people whose life and work bring them into immediate daily contact with suffering. True, there are the flashes of anger, the moments when heart and mind cry out why, why? What reason can there be for this monstrous pain, this anguish, this injustice? And yet, right in the midst of pain are the shafts of pure joy, the acts of generosity, of selflessness and of heroism which reveal the face of Christ.

It is my experience that those involved in caring, whether it be for alcoholics, drug addicts, the handicapped, the poor or the otherwise dispossessed, are called to a particular experience of Christ and his kingdom. They are called to share in his ministry of healing, of forgiveness, of the washing of feet — and in doing so they are caught up in the whole drama of redemptive suffering. This involvement can be like meeting a giant wave: it can catch you unawares so that you are bowled over and over, terrified, with your lungs full of water and mouth full of sand. Then after a while, if the ministry is right for you, you learn to cope with the sea. Sometimes you ride waves, sometimes you duck just in time, diving blindly into the dark water—and sometimes your timing is wrong and you get knocked over again. Then, just as you think "I've had it," you surface, amazed to find that you are still alive.

Let me share with you the poem from which I took these images of the sea. It was written by an American missionary sister whom I met in Chile, not long before I was arrested. She showed me the poem and I loved it so much that I copied it out and kept it in the pocket of the white coat that I wore at the hospital. When things were quiet I would take it out and read it again, pondering over what she meant. When I was arrested the poem remained safely in my locker at the hospital, and when the British consul offered to collect a few of my possessions to take back to England I asked him to look for the poem. He found it—the only one of my papers to escape the secret police. Now, I give it to you:

> I built my house by the sea.
> Not on the sands, mind you,
> not on the shifting sand.
> And I built it of rock.
> A strong house
> by a strong sea.
> And we got well acquainted, the sea and I.
> Good neighbors.
> Not that we spoke much.
> We met in silences,
> respectful, keeping our distance
> but looking our thoughts across the fence of sand.
> Always the fence of sand our barrier,
> always the sand between.
> And then one day
> (and I still don't know how it happened)

The sea came.
Without warning.
Without welcome even.
Not sudden and swift, but a shifting across the sand
    like wine.
Less like the flow of water than the flow of blood.
Slow, but flowing like an open wound.
And I thought of flight, and I thought of drowning,
    and I thought of death.
But while I thought the sea crept higher till it reached
    my door.
And I knew that there was neither flight nor death
    nor drowning.
That when the sea comes calling you stop being good
    neighbors,
well acquainted, friendly from a distance neighbors.
And you give your house for a coral castle
and you learn to breathe under water.

                            Carol Bialock

Now the curious thing is that all the time I was in Chile I understood the sea in this poem as an image of the presence of God —
the way he takes over our lives. When I showed it to a monk
friend, however, he saw the slow advance of the sea as the gradual encroachment of the agony of the world upon one's consciousness. It is only now, ten years on, that I begin to
understand what he meant when he said that the great mystery
is that the two are really the same.

⋊{ 2 }⋉

A Lover's Quarrel

Like Robert Frost's, a prophet's quarrel with the world is deep down a lover's quarrel. If they didn't love the world, they probably wouldn't bother to tell it that it is going to Hell. They'd just let it go. Their quarrel is God's quarrel.
(Frederick Buechner, *Wishful Thinking*)

In 1982 I moved my main professional locus from the cancer wards of Plymouth General Hospital to become the Medical Director of a small hospice for the dying. My work at the hospital already involved a good deal of terminal care so when I was offered the job at the hospice I did not see it as a dramatic change of direction. In the years that followed, however, I have become aware that the hospice has come to stand in prophetic relationship to the mainstream of medical care in our area. I should say at once that this role is neither conscious on the part of the hospice nor specifically articulated by anyone, but I believe that it is none the less true. Nor are we unique, for throughout the country hospices are having an effect upon medical thought and practice which is quite out of proportion to their size.

They are able to carry out this prophetic function because they fulfill three major criteria: they are drawn from the mainstream of society to live and work at one remove from it; they have the contemplative space to reflect upon the problems confronting them; and they do not choose this role but find them-

selves speaking a truth that they cannot contain. Like the
prophet Jeremiah, they complain bitterly:

> You have seduced me, Yahweh, and I have let myself
>   be seduced;
> you have overpowered me: you were the stronger . . .
> The word of Yahweh has meant for me
> insult, derision, all day long.
> I used to say, "I will not think about him,
> I will not speak his name any more."
> Then there seemed to be a fire burning in my heart,
> imprisoned in my bones.
> The effort to restrain it wearied me,
> I could not bear it.
>
> Jer. 20:7-9

In a consideration of the prophetic role of the hospice movement it is important to be clear on the meaning of the word
prophet, for it is often misused and therefore misunderstood.
Frederick Buechner, the American author of a pithy little book
of theological definitions called *Wishful Thinking,* writes:
"Prophet means *spokesman,* not fortune teller. The one whom
in their unfathomable audacity the prophet claimed to speak for
was the Lord and creator of the universe. There is no evidence
to suggest that anyone ever asked a prophet home for supper
more than once."

Prophets, then, are individuals or groups of people who are
called both to *listen* and to *speak out.* They must listen to God,
to the "signs of the times" and to the cries of the oppressed and
when they have understood the message, speak out, whatever
the personal cost. Prophets are no holier than anyone else. They
are frequently very wounded people — but like Jeremiah or Isaiah, they put their woundedness at the service of God. When
they hear the voice which says "Whom shall I send? Who will
be our messenger?" to their horror, they find themselves answering, "Here I am, send me" (Isa. 6:8).

Christians are familiar with the prophetic books of the
Hebrew Bible and the more poetic passages of Isaiah, Jeremiah,
Amos or Hosea are declaimed from many a cultured pulpit. It

is easy to domesticate the prophets in the same way that we tame the gospel and lose sight of how threatening what they said must have been to those who heard it. It cannot have been easy for Amos to pass this message from God on to his people:

> Trouble for those who are waiting so longingly for
>   the day of Yahweh! . . .
> I hate and despise your feasts,
> I take no pleasure in your solemn festivals.
> When you offer me holocausts, . . .
> I reject your oblations,
> and refuse to look at your sacrifices of fattened cattle.
> Let me have no more of the din of your chanting,
> no more of your strumming on harps.
> But let justice flow like water,
> and integrity like an unfailing stream.
>
>   Amos 5:18, 21-24

The fact is that prophetic messages are, almost by definition, unwelcome because they challenge the accepted status quo. As Buechner puts it: "The prophets were drunk, on God, and in the presence of their terrible tipsiness no one was ever comfortable. With a total lack of tact they roared out against phoniness and corruption wherever they found them. They were the terror of Kings and priests."

Today's prophets are just as tiresome. Amnesty International shouts its truth about imprisonment and torture from the housetops and persists in writing importunate letters to busy politicians and dictators. Greenpeace gets its silly rainbow boats in the way of important nuclear tests and the anti-smoking lobby keeps drawing attention to the five billion pound revenue the government receives from cigarette advertising. It is the same in the medical world. Just when the government is trying to tidy up the shambolic National Health Service and make it more efficient, health workers will go on about the emotional needs of the sick and ask for more resources for such tedious and unproductive groups as the elderly, the handicapped, and the dying.

I myself had a small David-like skirmish with the government

Goliaths a few years ago when they decided to reduce the nation's health bill by removing about 90 per cent of drugs from the list of those available on prescription. To do them justice it was, by and large, a sensible maneuver except that in their enthusiasm they removed a number of drugs which were vital to our use. One of these was a laxative which was the staple diet of expectant mothers and all patients who need strong narcotic drugs to remove their pain. Outraged, we protested. We gave interviews to the press, wrote letters to the government, all to no avail. Eventually ten of us doctors went to London for an interview with the Minister of Health and put our points as cogently and forcefully as we were able. Alas, we were no match for an experienced politician and he wriggled urbanely out of every attempt to pin him down so we returned home muttering darkly. Eventually, however, protest was so widespread that the drug was restored, so perhaps our efforts were not in vain.

Although it was exhausting, I have to admit that I rather enjoyed taking on the faceless giants of Westminster—especially when we won our cause! A much more difficult situation is to find oneself at odds with one's peers—the men and women one meets daily across the lunch table or in the hospital corridors. It happens, from time to time, that we at the hospice are involved in an unpleasant and painful conflict of loyalties between the needs of a particular patient and the unwritten rules of professional etiquette. It normally happens like this: a friend or relative of a patient rings the hospice to ask for help because someone is in pain or very distressed by the attitude of the doctors who are treating them in refusing to answer their questions openly. The medically correct answer to such a question is "I'm sorry there is nothing I can do. You must go back to your own doctor." If the distress is severe, however, it is not easy to behave "correctly" and one is faced with the difficult choice of confronting a colleague or maneuvering behind his back. It is always better to be open, of course, but this can lead to hard words and feelings because many doctors are very possessive of their patients and bitterly resent any interference from the outside.

It seems that this problem is one that will not go away, for despite our efforts to conform to the system people continue to beat a path to our door, seeking the help that they seemed unable to find elsewhere. Some of these callers are of course the sort who will always be dissatisfied, taking their troubles from doctor to doctor, unable to accept advice given to them or the fact that nothing can be done to help them. Leaving those sort of folk aside, there have been many that we have been able to help, needs that we have been able to meet, out of what are really quite limited resources. Let us look at some of the most common of these needs which, by their very existence, point to a flaw in the existing health services.

The first and most obvious thing for which people seek the help of a hospice is the relief of pain. Everyone is afraid of pain, and well they may be for it saps the strength and crowds the consciousness until the person is overwhelmed and wishes quite simply for death. Pain is very common (though not inevitable) in advanced cancer and yet in a hospice setting it nearly always comes rapidly under control. Why? Why is this not the case in hospital, and in the community? Do we have special instruments, techniques which are not available to ordinary people? The answer, absurdly, is no. We use the same drugs, the same techniques and practically no high-tech medicine. It is a question of experience in diagnosis and in the handling of a few very common drugs and of a meticulous attention to detail. More than anything it is an attitude which says pain is soul destroying and unnecessary and we will not rest until it is relieved.

Put like that, it sounds so self-righteous. I do not mean it to be so. I am just as ignorant in other areas of medicine as some of my colleagues are about pain control in the dying. That is why we are specialists. My complaint is not against individual doctors but rather against a system of government which spends money on weapons or tax relief for the rich while people in public hospitals lie curled up in pain which could be relieved.

But distress in the dying is not only about pain and unpleasant symptoms, but about much more fundamental issues such as the inappropriate prolongation of poor quality life and a way of treating people which is, quite unintentionally, terribly hurtful. One of the things which has become very clear to me over the past few years is that, in some situations, doctors get trapped into prolonging the life of people who, frankly, wish they were dead. The reasons for this are very complex, but let me attempt to unravel them. A woman gets, say, cancer of the ovary. She has an operation to remove the growth and then chemotherapy to try and eradicate the malignant cells. So far, so good. She goes into remission and is well and happy for the next two years. Then the growth comes back. This time the doctors know from experience with other patients that they cannot cure her. They try to buy more time with other anti-cancer drugs but she feels terrible and the drugs do no good. She loses weight and strength so that she can no longer get about on her own. Then the tumor causes a blockage in her bowels. What should the doctors do then? Do they operate and perhaps give her another month of life, or do they relieve her pain and discomfort and let her "die in dignity" without I-V's and tubes and a colostomy? They must weigh up the needs of an individual patient. An elderly widow may dread more than anything the indignity of surgery and dependence upon relatives who do not want her, while a married couple may be prepared to pay any price for a few extra weeks together. One cannot lay down the law, only state the basic principle that each patient has a right to be treated as an individual and be given the choice about whether or not they want invasive treatment to prolong their life. It is only by being open with people about their situation that one can learn that, in the vast majority of situations, quality of life is more important than numerical length of days.

All this seems so obvious. What then goes wrong? Why is anti-cancer treatment pushed to seemingly outrageous limits or elderly people submitted to major surgery when they wish that their lives would peacefully end? One of the great dilemmas for doctors is that much of the time they are working at the frontiers of cancer medicine, using drugs which have a 10, 20 or 30 per cent chance of cure. If the drug works they are heroes and bouquets are given—while if they fail everyone mutters that it was criminal that the person was put through so much suffering and died anyway. I thank God that I do not have to make these decisions.

Another factor however is that as doctors we are trained from the cradle to fight disease and to save life. It is instinctive, deep rooted, second nature. Disease is the enemy and death the ultimate disaster. When our patients get better we feel good, affirmed, fulfilled. When they die we feel bad, guilty, a failure. Now in many ways this conditioning is a good thing: it spurs us on to work appalling hours and exhaust ourselves in the struggle to save life. It pulls us out of bed at three in the morning to deliver babies or patch up drunk drivers; it drives us on to work on automatic pilot when head and heart are too exhausted to care if the patient lives or dies. How then can we be expected to change gear and allow nature to take its course, to raise the white flag, to give way to the enemy?

Of course, we must and we do: but it is not easy. Pneumonia, hemorrhage, dehydration, the classic modes of death are all amenable to treatment, even if their underlying causes are not. We have to learn a new way of practicing medicine, a staying of the hand, allowing people to die a gentle death today instead of resuscitating them to live another painful week or die a more difficult death tomorrow. And of course if we are to stay our hand rather than fight on we must explain why—to the family, to the nurses, to our colleagues, perhaps even to our patients. We may not be understood, we may be blamed, we may even be sued. It is not easy to stop treatment; it is so much easier to do battle, to keep fighting, so that when death comes in spite of our I-V's and tubes and machines the bystanders will say, "The doctors were wonderful. They did everything they could."

Slowly we are learning that the wielding of our high-tech guns is not to be equated with doing everything possible. This involves a different approach, a treating of the whole person, a negotiation and consultation and a tailoring of treatment to the individual. It involves making ourselves available to answer people's questions, sitting by the bedside, drawing diagrams, talking to angry relatives and above all admitting that we have no power to cure—that we are not God. And of course, it involves the learning of new skills: how to handle old drugs differently and how to communicate more effectively. It involves making fools of ourselves with role-play and video feedback, learning that we do badly what we thought we did superbly well. And worst of all it involves allowing our citadel to be breached by those we used to perceive as tiresome charlatans: the practitioners of alternative medicine. We have to learn to sift out the useful paramedical treatments from the magic, discarding the coffee enemas but holding on to and evaluating the usefulness of meditation, relaxation, and psychotherapy. We have to learn to be whole-person doctors because our patients are whole persons. It takes so much more time and energy. It is destroying our protective hierarchies, our sense of omnipotence. Our corridors of power have been invaded and we are having to learn humility!

Another area in which we at the hospice find ourselves in the role of advocate is the way in which patients are liable to be treated as objects, rather than people. Perhaps I should rephrase this, for neither I nor my colleagues would ever consider a patient as an "object." What happens is that, for a number of very complex reasons, doctors and nurses sometimes treat people in a way that makes them *feel* as if they are considered as objects. That this is so there can be no doubt. I have experienced it myself and I have heard the complaint from many patients. The nicest quote on the subject comes from a woman who died in our hospice a couple of years ago; she spoke angrily of the junior hospital doctors as "underlings who argue about you as they go by." Poor H., she was spitting with fury. The junior doctors would have been amazed at her perception of them for they were working to help her, struggling to understand the disease processes and how best to relieve her suffering. I believe that there are three major causes of this misunderstanding between doctors and their patients and although it would be difficult to resolve it altogether, much can be done to lessen it and the dissatisfaction that ensues.

The first problem lies in "the system" — the need for efficiency in dealing with large numbers of patients. This problem has been with us for a long time and it is difficult to imagine that it will go away. If we are to use resources and equipment efficiently, then people must attend clinics together, be registered in a ledger and so on. Unfortunately, they must usually wait to see a doctor because it is impossible to predict how long a given consultation will take and we must see as many people as need to be seen. Most people take this in their stride. What they do find hard, however, is the depersonalizing treatment of being stripped and put into hospital dressing gowns before they see the doctor. A patient coming up to see the doctor for the first time will, consciously or unconsciously, dress themselves in such a way as to present themselves as they would wish to be seen. Their clothes are body language which declare who they are, individual people with their own tastes and ideas. If we ask people to remove their clothes and put on a uniform *before* they meet the doctor, we are removing from them some of the protective armor they need for this difficult interview. We are in fact depersonalizing them, treating them as objects, and we make them less able to communicate effectively because they are nervous and embarrassed.

In the same way, if a third party is present at a medical consultation, the patient is frequently inhibited. It matters nothing that the third party is a nurse, that she is a professional and that she is friendly: her presence will alter the interaction between doctor and patient and reduce the communication. Why then, do we do it? Mostly, of course, we are trying to cram an impossible workload into too small a space of time. The second reason is that most doctors are quite unaware of the emotional discomfort of their patients. They are polite and friendly and the patient smiles back and all seems well. It is only when you ask people how they felt about the consultation that the truth emerges: that many people are angry, humiliated or in other ways dissatisfied with the way they have been treated. There is, however, a third issue which is very much more subtle, and therefore both fascinating and threatening; the question of "distancing." By "distancing" I mean the way in which doctors and nurses, quite unconsciously, keep patients at arm's length so that they, the carers, can cope with the constant daily contact with suffering. Distancing happens in two ways: one is the way we organize health care and the other is in the way we handle a given interaction with a patient. The first way, involving the system, I will examine here, the second in Chapter 8.

To understand distancing we need to start from a basic premise: life is unfair, and for many people very cruel indeed. We all know that because we have family, friends, and neighbors and because we either read the papers, listen to the radio or watch television. Most people, however, have only a limited contact with suffering. Their parents die, perhaps a friend gets killed in a motorcycle accident or someone at work gets cancer. They are

touched by it for a while but then life goes back to "normal."
For doctors, nurses, social workers and other health care workers, however, contact with suffering *is* normal. Every day I see
men and women whose lives have been disrupted by incurable
cancer. Many of them are completely devastated. Couples who
have loved each other to the exclusion of anyone else are suddenly separated; mothers of tiny children wither and die linger-
ing, mutilated deaths, trapped day and night with the fetid
tumors that replace mouth or breast or genitals. It is indeed
cruel and we find it very hard.

How then do we, the carers, cope? We cope in a number of
different ways. The most important is that we are skilled in our
jobs so we do whatever is necessary to treat the sick. Being able
to do something is a marvelous protection from pain. The other
thing that happens is that we create a professional distance
between the client and ourselves. We wear a uniform that gives
us status and protection. We see them on *our* territory so that
we feel comfortable and in control. We see them with a colleague — another doctor or a nurse — so that the encounter is
formalized and contained. And we see them partially stripped
of their identity so that we meet them as *patients,* not as friends
and neighbors.

Now I am not saying for a moment that any of these things
is wrong; just noting that they separate and therefore protect
me from the suffering of the other person which threatens to
overwhelm me. The converse of all this is to meet someone
suffering on *their* territory, alone and when you are impotent to
help. That is when it really hurts: when you share their pain
instead of relieving it. That is very costly and we can only take
a little of it.

The reality of the caring situation is that we alter the variables
to the needs of the patient and what we can handle at any given
moment. When I am feeling strong I see patients alone, without
my white coat and ask them how they are *feeling* not only physically but emotionally. I ask them if they are afraid, if they are
sad or if they are angry and I ask them how things are at home.
This takes time and a lot of emotional energy and I cannot do
it for every patient, so I do it for those who seem to need it

most. By doing this I am meeting a small fraction of the human needs of the sick for whom I care.

On the days when I am not feeling very strong I see people more formally, with a nurse at my side. I ask them about their physical symptoms and check the progress of the disease. I order investigations, prescribe treatment and then go away and see someone else. That is the way things are. We too are human and, as Eliot says, humankind cannot bear too much reality.

So what is the prophetic hospice movement saying to mainstream medicine? Perhaps, like the prophets of old, we are the spokespersons for the oppressed. We listen to the cries of the people and try to speak out for them. We relate that they want to be treated as normal responsible people. They want to have their illness explained to them in words that they can understand and to be consulted about its treatment. They want to retain their dignity as individuals and keep some control over their lives. They want to participate in their care and share in our decision-making. They want us to be honest with them, warm and humble. More than anything, they want us to combine our competence with compassion and, when our hands are empty, to stay our ground and share the frightening darkness with them. More than anything, they need our *love*.

{ 3 }

ROOM FOR LOVING

There is room in the world for loving;
there is no room for hate.
There is room in the world for sharing;
there is no room for greed.
There is room for justice;
no room for privilege.
There is room for compassion;
no room for pride.

John Harriott
Our World

In the previous chapter I wrote of the prophetic role of the hospice movement and one of my favorite and most tantalizing intellectual games is trying to identify what it is that makes the hospice where I work so different from the hospital. (I should add that this is a dangerous game which many people play and in which the inexperienced can be badly hurt, because comparisons are both misleading and invidious.) Hospices, like all prophets, are called from the mainstream of society to live their truth on the periphery. Sometimes their lifestyle brings them bouquets; sometimes they are pelted with rotten eggs. Perhaps even the balance of these is crucial for too much praise can corrupt while too little can dishearten and destroy.

What is it that makes hospices—all hospices—so different from hospitals? Surely the ingredients are the same: doctors, nurses, patients, beds, machines—all these are to be found wherever the sick are cared for. The difference lies in the way these elements are blended together or, to use another image, in the way that the players in the drama relate to each other. These relations are different because the *philosophy* of hospices is different. It is a philosophy based upon the conviction that people, all people, however far gone, are infinitely precious and their treatment must be tailored to their individual needs. We are treating not just a case of breast cancer, but a woman called Mary, her husband John, and their children, Sally and David. Here we get to the heart of the matter: the dying are individuals, complex human beings whose needs are legion: physical, intellectual, emotional, spiritual, social. In hospital we provide high quality treatment to the tip of the human iceberg: we diagnose disease and try to cure it. We attend to the basic physical needs as well as our resources permit. We are as patient and kind as we are able to be given the shortage of personnel and the pressures of work. We try to help the families when they are in difficulty, but mostly, we dare not open the Pandora's box of human fear and anguish. We are not encouraged to ask people what it *really* feels like to have cancer, to be dying. We are not taught to hold their hands when they are lonely or afraid, or to cradle them sobbing in our arms, smoothing the hair, holding them until the paroxysms pass. We are not trained to *love*. Or rather we are trained to *suppress* our love, to don a protective uniform especially for work: a uniform that keeps us at a safe distance from our patients so that our meetings are those of professional and client, not of the frail human beings that we all are.

Could it be that we are unconsciously denying our patients the one thing that they long for, the one gift that it is in our power to give: our human warmth?

To love tenderly: how sweetly the phrase rolls off the tongue, conjuring up images of nurses smoothing fevered brows and fatherly doctors comforting weeping relatives. In the world of the terminally ill, "TLC"—tender loving care—does indeed involve this and a good deal more besides. In exploring the spirituality of the carer we need to look no further than the gospels, for the pattern of Jesus' loving provides a model for our own. It confirms our twentieth-century intuition that loving is a costly business demanding a radical renunciation of human distaste and prejudice, a gift of self which is often more than we had bargained for. If the sugar-sweet comforting image of the gentle Jesus is a tawdry piece of kitsch masking the harsh and terrible love of our God made human, so too is a sentimental concept of those who care for the dying.

Love, especially in the hospice context, can be a very practical and earthly business. I think especially of David, a bachelor in his late forties who is a patient in the hospice as I write.

David is a wonderful man, one of the poor of our successful affluent society who has lost even the one possession that remained to him: his physical integrity. By the time he was referred to our service, the cancer in his mouth had recurred despite treatment and he had a painful malignant ulcer where his teeth should have been. I saw him regularly in my outpatient clinic, always accompanied by a young psychiatric community nurse who cared for him, but he refused admission, jealously guarding his independence despite a growing terror of choking to death. On Christmas day he gave in and came to spend the day with us. Never will I forget the moment when he handed me a bottle of champagne and a torn scrap of paper on which he scribbled, "I appreciate all that you're doing for me." I asked him if he could manage a little liquified turkey and was hard-pressed not to cry when he said, "Thank you, but a little watery porridge will be fine."

"A little watery porridge, thank you." His words went round and round in my mind all day, as I cooked and ate the Christmas feast with the various members of my family. How indeed could I banish from my thoughts the man whose mouth was full not of Christmas food, but of a foul necrotic tumor?

We all thought David must die soon, and indeed so did he, but in the perverse way of tumors of the face, although he was horribly mutilated there was nothing to actually kill him. Today, as I write, two months have elapsed and he is still alive, a gaunt figure crouched before the television, clutching his tissues and vomit bowl, mercifully oblivious of the appalling stench from his tumor which fills the room. It is difficult to explain the love-hate relationships we have with these specters at the feast of life. We are not immune to the smell of decaying flesh, and like anyone, we long to escape to where the air is pure. We too are unable to understand his mumbled words and must kneel patiently by his chair as he struggles to write a few phrases on his note pad. We have long since admitted to each other that we wish his suffering could end. And yet alongside this wish, cohabiting peacefully with our distaste, is a real love for this broken man. We have come to value his humor and respect his courage, and like Professor Higgins, we've grown accustomed to his face. We are proud that he feels sufficiently at home with us to leave the privacy of his room and expose his disfigured face in the dining room where all the world passes by. People mutter of him, as of others, "How awful. If it was a dog, you'd have it put to sleep." True. But then David is not a dog, but a man with cancer in his mouth, who is living out his last precarious days among friends, loved and cherished in a way that he has never known before. His is the experience described in this poem by Sidney Carter: the one surprise of being loved:

> No revolution will come in time
> to alter this man's life
> except the one surprise
> of being loved.
> He has no interest in Civil Rights
> neo-marxism
> psychiatry
> or any kind of sex.
> He has only twelve more hours to live so never mind
>   about
> a cure for cancer, smoking, leprosy
> or osteoarthritis.
> Over this dead loss to society
> you pour your precious ointment,
> call the bluff
> and laugh at the
> fat and clock-faced gravity
> of our economy.
> You wash the feet that

will not walk tomorrow.
Come levity of love,
Show him, show me
in this last step of time
Eternity, leaping and capering.

It is in this lavishing of love on patients like David that the hospice movement stands in a prophetic relationship to society at large, for it affirms the value of the brain-damaged, the mutilated and the old to a world which values the clever, the physically beautiful and the athlete. Only recently I spent the afternoon with a young French doctor who, when I took him to see our new hospice, still under construction, exclaimed, "I never before imagined that someone would build a place which is specially designed to provide comfort for the dying."

What I am arguing for here when I talk about love is not for more hospices or more time spent at work but about a set of attitudes. It is about developing a degree of insight into the patient's world—what the psychologists call empathy. With that insight goes a heightened sensitivity to the patient's distress and a searching for ways to relieve it—or at least not to make it worse. At heart, professional loving is about competence, empathy and communication. It is about becoming sensitive to the pain of others and therefore terribly vulnerable. For me, as for many, it is a way of caring which I aspire to, but achieve only some of the time. It is a costly loving for which I am repaid a hundredfold.

One of the most sensitive issues in professional caring is "becoming involved" with the person we are caring for, the patient, or in psychological jargon, "the client." There is no standard teaching on "how far one can go" in professional loving, and indeed any one carer will probably work differently with different people and at different times, depending on the time and personal resources available.

My own involvement with caring for the terminally ill in the hospice "style" has led me in a particular medical direction, which ten years ago I would not have dreamed of. After qualifying as a doctor I embarked upon a career as a surgeon. I am good with my hands and planned to use my skill in treating hand injuries and burns, cancer and congenital deformities. To put it another way, I was a "body" doctor who enjoyed reducing fractures, suturing wounds and generally patching up broken people. It simply did not occur to me to explore how my patients *felt* about their illness: my job lay in the diagnosis and healing of bodily ills and my psychiatric colleagues would take care of the depressed and psychotic. Psychology I wrote off in my youthful arrogance as being nothing more than common sense, which I thought I had in plenty. I blush now to think of my ignorance — though I know my life was less complicated and my work less costly before it dawned upon me that good medicine demands care of the whole person, body, mind and spirit.

The doctor specializing in terminal care is usually referred the cases where "there is nothing more to be done" — where surgery, radiotherapy and anti-cancer drugs are either inappropriate from the outset or have ceased to do any good. In practice (mercifully for our self-esteem and professional survival) there nearly always is something more physical to be done: a fine tuning of pain control or drug manipulation to alleviate unpleasant symptoms. When this is done, however, we are in the same position as our colleagues — empty-handed. What we have to do then is learn to work with these empty hands: to use them for comforting and healing of a different kind. A certain proportion of this kind of work is what is known as counseling: a skilled listening and interpretation of psychological problems and distress. This is what psychologists and psychotherapists and professional counselors do. Even among these small professional groups there are differences of theory and personal style but all of them think in terms of therapist and client: it is a professional relationship based on the psychological needs of one person and the skilled response of another to those needs. The distance between them is integral both to the success of treatment and the survival of the carer.

Psychological work with the terminally ill has many of the features of other types of counseling and psychotherapy but the relationship is changed by two factors: the first is the shortness of the clients' expected life span and the second is the enormity of their loss. In my experience, and I am neither psychotherapist nor trained counselor, those facing death have a particularly urgent need of human warmth and honest straightforward communication. My personal "style" has evolved over eight years of work in the field and is characterized by a degree of directness and informality that is unusual in ordinary medical practice. In ten years I have changed from being rather shy about physical contact to being quite at home holding patients' hands or letting them weep on my shoulder. I find that this physical aspect of comforting flows very naturally from honest communication about painful truths and is in no way dependent upon length of relationship. Perhaps I can illustrate this with a typical scenario.

It happens quite frequently that I am asked to see a patient in one of the surgical wards of our big district hospital. The referral may be to consider the patient for admission to the hospice or just to advise on his pain and symptom control. Not uncommonly I am asked to help out because the patient is having difficulty coming to terms with his diagnosis or because the family has forbidden the doctors to tell him the truth about his illness and tensions are arising out of the deception.

One thing I have learned is that these encounters should not be conducted when I am under severe time constraints or very tired. I now feel free to ring the ward and say, "I'm sorry, I'm at the end of my rope tonight. Will it be OK if I come tomorrow? I'll do it much better." If the need is urgent I will go anyway, but if not I will leave it until I am better able to work with sensitivity. When I go to the ward I always ask the nurses about the patient before I see him or her. The nurses are usually much closer to the patient than his doctors and are often more aware of his hopes and fears. But when I ask them "does he know?" — meaning, of course, does he know he has cancer and that he is going to die — they often look at each other and say, "I think he knows, don't you? — but he doesn't say anything."

Then, armed with as much information as possible, I arrange to see the person on their own. "This often takes a bit of organizing, but I have learned to my cost that "heavy" conversations behind curtains can have a disturbing effect on the other patients who are inevitably sitting with their ears pricked to catch even the whispered confidences. Having the courage and authority to insist that a patient be put in a wheel-chair and taken into the office or, if bed bound, wheeled, bed and all, into a side ward is crucial, not only because of the importance of other patients not hearing but because both the interviewer and the patient are severely constrained in what they say by knowledge that someone else is listening. (One of the difficulties for nurses working in the community is that they do not feel they have the authority to insist that a relative leave the room while they talk to the patient, so they struggle with the problems of communication in a three-cornered conversation in which an over-protective spouse often answers for a patient quite capable of speaking for him or herself.)

Once alone with a new patient I introduce myself, explain that I have come at the request of their doctor, and ask them to tell me their story. The fact that I am familiar with the history and diagnosis makes no difference to this maneuver for its purpose is not to inform me of things which I already know but to establish a rapport and to elicit some of the submerged iceberg material of sadness and anger. It is in the telling of the story that I meet my patients and in my listening to them that they meet me. This first meeting is a pivotal one in establishing a therapeutic relationship and it may take up to an hour—sometimes longer. But it is time well spent for in that hour one can establish bonds of trust and confidence which are the practical tools for later "work." Everything depends on the quality of my listening: the patients must understand clearly from my verbal and non-verbal cues that I am interested in them as persons as well as in their physical problems. This means not only paying careful attention as they speak, but asking them to clarify issues which I do not understand. As their story unfolds I make notes and if it does not emerge spontaneously, I ask not only what happened and what the doctors said to them but how they felt about it then—and how they feel now. This exploration of the emotional as well as the physical component of the cancer journey is the key to establishing a supportive relationship. It is often the first time a patient has been asked by a doctor—or indeed by anyone—how they feel about things and they may well begin to cry.

It is at this stage of the dialogue that the doctor, or other worker, may further affirm the patient's worth and forge bonds between them. Patients are nearly always embarrassed and ashamed if they cry in front of the doctor—and many doctors find it hard to cope with. I well remember a surgical colleague who, when a patient began to weep in a clinic, put his finger on her nose in a jocular fashion, "Now, now Iris, we don't want any of *that,* do we?" When a patient weeps with me, I draw a little closer to them and perhaps put a hand on their shoulder. I tell them that they must feel free to cry—that they have every right to be sad or angry or confused. This "permission" to cry is only a permission to be a human person and indulge in what is a very normal and therapeutic release of emotion. When the tears have passed, and they usually do in a few minutes, the person nearly always feels better and somehow comforted, albeit by a stranger.

It sometimes happens during the course of such an interview, that a patient asks me if his illness can be cured. This is *the question*—feared by so many carers and so often answered with evasive platitudes or outright lies. I prefer to leave the issue of telling the truth about diagnosis until later; but I may say at this juncture that clear, direct questions about a patient's diagnosis and future *always* deserve an honest answer. It is never right to lie. This does not mean that one should ever be brutal with the truth. One must listen carefully to what the patient is asking and respond slowly, one step at a time, monitoring the response and stopping when it appears that they have enough to absorb for the moment. The "art" of breaking bad news is one we all need to learn and it should be adequately taught to all doctors and nurses in training.

As always we return to the two essential components of good caring: competence and compassion. Well-meant kindness is not enough, nor are the most carefully learned communication skills: but the two together can transform despair into hope, neurotic demanding behavior into marvelous dignity and courage.

It is curious how this phrase "dying with dignity" has crept into modern language about the care of the dying. I find it rather tiresome, conjuring up stereotypical images of people breathing their last in calm, hushed surroundings, with nurses and family tiptoeing in and out of darkened rooms. I now understand dignity in a rather different way which has more to do with integrity of personality than external order and serenity. One of the most important aspects of my work is helping people cope with impending death by exploring their fears, debunking the myths and facing the real ones truthfully with them. It is ironic that most "undignified" or "neurotic" behavior in those facing death is the result of the way they have been handled by their carers.

A short time ago, while working with a colleague in the hospital outpatients department, I saw two middle-aged women who were behaving in a very undignified fashion, being aggressive, demanding, and apparently unreasonable. Each was like a bomb on point of detonation, possessed by anger and discontent with the world in general and their doctors in particular. By coincidence we had had a run of deaths at the hospice and I had several empty beds so I offered to take the ladies in to "sort them out." My colleague was a little surprised as neither of them could be considered "terminal," but was grateful to have the problem taken off his hands. I admitted both women directly from the clinic and stood back to watch the sparks fly. By the time I arrived back at the hospice they were in and already there was trouble. Kate's daughter met me at the top of the stairs to say that Mary had not stopped talking since she arrived and was driving her mother mad. I looked in the neat three-bedded ward and there was a very tense Kate perched miserably on the edge of her chair while Mary gave vent to her feelings from the adjacent bed. Luckily the bed in our single ward was temporarily empty while its occupant was at home for a couple of days; and so, lying in my teeth, I asked Kate if she would do me a great favor by changing to another room, and taking her gently by the arm I steered her out of earshot of Mary's diatribe.

Over the next two weeks the nurses, my fellow doctors, and I "worked" with Kate and Mary. Ninety per cent of this consisted of being a sounding board, listening patiently and attentively while they told and retold the tale of their illnesses. These were all-too-familiar stories of fear and anxiety, magnified out of all proportion by medical collusion. Kate was the angriest. She was a chronic bronchitic who had nursed several of her elder sisters through terminal illness and then fallen sick herself. Suspecting the worst, she had asked her doctors outright whether she had cancer. "They patted me on the head, like a little girl," she said, "and told me not to worry." But Kate did worry. Her "bronchitis" did not seem to be getting any better and she was not responding to antibiotics in the way she used to. Eventually she was unable to cope alone and decided to go and stay with her daughter in Plymouth. The consultant gave her a sealed letter to give to the doctor who would be taking over her care. Safely at home Kate looked at the envelope and then, no doubt looking furtively to right and left, she opened it. Inside she found a letter which spoke of an elderly woman with an advanced incurable lung cancer who would soon need terminal care. "The daughter knows, but we decided it would be better not to tell the patient," she read. Kate was not only furious but humiliated. It was her body and her life—and yet here were these people considering to keep her in the dark, treating her as if she were a child or already totally incompetent. It is little wonder that when she came to our clinic she was not the archetypal polite, deferential, grateful patient. Poor Kate! It was her carers who had robbed her of her dignity. Two days later, it was a very different woman who sat on the hospice lawn stroking Trudy, my assistant Michael's dog, and posing with a smile for the TV cameras who happened to be filming the hospice that day. By now Kate knew she had cancer and that she was going to die—but she had control of her life again. It was her decision to stay in the hospice—and her decision two weeks later to spend £300 and risk shortening her life by going to London in a taxi to say goodbye to her friends.

The hard part for Kate will be the gradual relinquishing of her independence. Fiery spirits like hers find it very difficult to accept the loss of their freedom to move about unaided and ultimately the weakness that makes it impossible even to change position in bed. As Kate becomes weaker the burden upon her daughter will increase. She will need enormous patience to cope with the frustration of not being able to help and the sadness of seeing her mother fail. If only for her daughter's sake I hope that when Kate's time does come she is in ours or some other hospice, for her daughter will need all the help she can get to cope with her mother's anger and her own impotence and guilt.

I do not pretend, of course, that the hospice world has a monopoly on skilled and loving care. One can find the same quality of care in many different situations: in a general hospital, in homes for the mentally handicapped, units for drug addiction or in services for the treatment of patients with AIDS. I think in particular of L'Arche communities or of my friends Benedict and Lila who share their home with a number of young schizophrenics. Benedict is an Orthodox priest and he and his wife Lila have eight children. For twenty years they have opened their home to people in need and for the past ten years this has meant young schizophrenics from the locked wards of psychiatric hospitals. Patients apparently uncontainable in a traditional institution become somehow tamed in their home, joining in the life of the family and watching the miracle of lambs being born. Lest we get carried away with sentimentality and the beauty of this vision, however, let me quote the conversation that I had with Benedict when I first spoke to him on the telephone. "Today," he said, "is my fiftieth birthday, and I have spent it scraping shit off the bedroom wall!"

I knew then that we were kindred spirits, for the only kind of holiness I can cope with is that which is firmly grounded in reality. As I said before, loving is a costly business and one needs an earthy sense of humor to survive. This poem by an English Benedictine monk is one of my favorites, for it has no illusions about the pain of discipleship:

> Anoint the wounds
> of my spirit
> with the balm
> of forgiveness.
> Pour the oil
> of your calm
> upon the waters
> of my heart.
> Take the squeal
> of frustration
> from the wheels of my passion
> that the power
> of your tenderness
> may smooth
> the way I love.
> That the tedium

of giving
in the risk of surrender
and the reaching
out naked
to a world
that must wound
may be kindled fresh daily
in a blaze of compassion
—that the grain may fall gladly
to burst in the ground
—and the harvest abound.

Ralph Wright

⊰{ 4 }⊱

A NEW COMMANDMENT

My little children . . .
I give you a new commandment:
love one another . . .
John 13:33-34

In the next few chapters I will be exploring the manner of Jesus' loving as shown in some of the familiar gospel stories. But before I embark upon the New Testament teaching, I would like to look back for a moment to the Old Testament understanding of love. Why, I wonder, did Jesus say that his command to love was *new?* He and his disciples were steeped in the Jewish scriptures and must have been deeply familiar with the teaching of God's tenderness and predilection for the poor, the suffering, and the oppressed. Throughout the Old Testament runs the theme of *Hesed,* the faithful covenant love of God for his people. We meet it first in Exodus, in the marvelous stories of Moses' encounters with God on Mount Sinai. True, God tells Moses that he may neither know God's name nor see God's face, but in amazing, scary moments in the cloud, when all the Israelites are cowering in their tents, God is revealed. "Yahweh, Yahweh, a God of tenderness and compassion, slow to anger, rich in kindness and faithfulness" (Exod. 34:6). I love the rich counterpoint between images of the mysterious unknowable God of Sinai and the God who is tender and full of compassion. In Hosea we find the same message expressed in different, more poetic imagery. The prophet likens God to a father besotted with love for his child, loving him unconditionally, in spite of neglect and rejection:

> When Israel was a child I loved him,
> and I called my son out of Egypt.
> But the more I called to them, the further they went
> from me . . .
> I led them with reins of kindness,
> with leading strings of love.
> I was like someone who lifts an infant
> close against his cheek;
> stooping down to him I gave him his food.
>
> Hos. 11:1-4

It is worth exploring for a minute the richness of meaning in the Hebrew word *Hesed,* which is variously translated as mercy, (loving) kindness, steadfast love, constancy, loyalty. This is the word which is translated as *love tenderly* in the passage from Micah 6, which I have used as a framework for understanding the demands on the carer, and it appears again in the lines from Exodus quoted above. The interesting thing about this word is that although it refers primarily to God's relationship with the people, to God's faithfulness within the covenant relationship, it applies also to *the people's* reciprocal covenant obligation to God and to each other.

A covenant is by its nature a relationship, a bond between two parties, and God's loyalty to the promise to protect and sustain God's people in times of hardship and distress laid upon them the obligation to support each other, especially the weaker members of the community:

> It is he who sees justice done for the orphan and the widow, who loves the stranger and gives him food and clothing. Love the stranger then, for you were strangers in the land of Egypt. It is Yahweh your God you must fear and serve; you must cling to him; in his name take your oaths. (Deut. 10:18-20)

These themes of God's love for the people and the demand that they should care for one another run throughout the books of the Old Testament. They emerge with special power and clarity in the books of the prophets, especially the eighth-century writers Amos, Hosea, Isaiah, and Micah, as they denounce injustice and ritual worship by those who oppress the poor. Like Amos, Isaiah was outspoken in his condemnation of those whose secret lives were at odds with their religious observance:

> What are your endless sacrifices to me?
> says Yahweh. . . .
> When you stretch out your hands
> I turn my eyes away.
> You may multiply your prayers,
> I shall not listen.
> Your hands are covered with blood,
> wash, make yourselves clean.
> Take your wrong doing out of my sight.
> Cease to do evil.
> Learn to do good,
> search for justice,
> help the oppressed,
> be just to the orphan,
> plead for the widow.
>
> Isa. 1:11, 15-17

It is tempting to read this as a quaint invective against the people of a past age, but it requires no great leap of the imagination to apply it to, for example, a Mass of thanksgiving to celebrate the anniversary of a military coup, such as was held until recently each year in the Chilean capital, Santiago. Sermons such as this are indeed preached in our own times. Men like Archbishop Helder Camara of Brazil and South African Bishop Desmond Tutu have survived to be a thorn in the flesh of a repressive government. Others, like Martin Luther King or Poland's Father Jerzy Popieluszko have died a martyr's death because their love drove them to speak out against injustice. El Salvador's Archbishop Oscar Romero was assassinated as he celebrated Mass just two days after he told his people:

> No soldier is obliged to obey an order contrary to the law of God. Nobody has to fulfil an immoral law. Now it is

time that you recover your consciences and that you first obey your conscience rather than an order to sin. The church, defender of the rights of God, of the human dignity of the person, cannot remain shut up before such an abomination. We want the government to take seriously that reforms achieved with so much blood serve no one. In the name of God, then, and in the name of this suffering people, whose cries rise to the heavens, every day more clamoringly, I beg you, I ask you, I order you in the name of God: stop the repression.

It would be easy to comfort ourselves that we of the peaceful nations give our tithes to the church and to charities like Oxfam and Amnesty International and that our hands are clean. But alas, life is not quite so simple. The book that I use for my night prayers reminds me uncomfortably of the sins of an affluent society which I so conveniently forget: that most of the time I am quite blind to need and suffering outside my immediate circle; that I give no more than a passing thought to pollution, erosion and acid rain, and that quite frankly my concern is with the here and now, not for those who will follow me in the next generation. Like the rest of the nation, I share in the corporate guilt of arms production, in the hypocrisy that wails over natural disasters like earthquakes while scientists in their laboratories prostitute their intelligence and training by making weapons that could destroy us all. Again, like the rest of my fellow citizens, I live my life in complicity with the exploitation of the peoples who produce the raw materials for the things which sustain my very comfortable existence. All this and so much more. As John Harriott puts it:

> We should be in mourning,
> we should be in tears,
> our blinds perpetually drawn.
> We are to be lords of the earth,
> not of each other.
>   from *Our World*

Let whoever is without sin throw the first stone! When the knowledge of my own infidelity makes me sick at heart, I turn to the prayers set for Thursday:

Loving God, close your eyes to our sins . . .
Make us whole, steadfast in spirit.
Broken are our bones, yet you can heal us
and we shall leap for joy and dance again.
Jim Cotter from *Prayer at Night*

Jim Cotter's prayers have a special power both because of their poetry and their understanding of human weakness. It is not easy to rebuke without humiliating, to condemn sin without leaving the sinner in despair. Just as the carer must hold death and resurrection in the same paschal overview, so must the pastor hold correction, forgiveness, and hope together in one package, so that the consciousness of woundedness and sin is not the burden that crushes us, but rather the impulse to a change of heart. This is the essence of Christian pastoral ministry, the new commandment of Jesus:

I give you a new commandment:
love one another;
just as I have loved you,
you also must love one another.
By this love you have for one another,
everyone will know that you are my disciples.
John 13:34-35

Love one another
JUST AS I HAVE LOVED YOU.

Here we have a new dimension to an old law. Jesus' disciples must not only be just to the oppressed, give food to the hungry, and shelter the homeless poor. They must go that extra mile, turn the other cheek and hand over their trousers to the man who demands their jacket. Jesus' disciples are invited to make a unilateral declaration of love on strangers and enemies — for even corrupt businessmen and military dictators are good to their friends! This is why I spoke of the harsh and terrible love of our God made human — and why so many of us, like the rich young man, find the words of the gospel too hard and either turn sadly away or try to water down its demands. As the Benedictine monk Tom Cullinan puts it:

> The trouble is that we have taken hold of a stallion and we have domesticated it into a sort of riding-school pony: but the gospel is really a stallion that cannot be domesticated. (*The Roots of Social Justice*)

⊰{ 5 }⊱

SAMARITAN OR LEVITE

When someone asks me what Christianity is all about,
it is the one parable in the Gospels
that I think about
because I think
this is it.

Christopher William Jones
Listen Pilgrim

To love tenderly — Micah's second blueprint for discipleship:
how simple a command yet how difficult to obey, for the suffering are a bottomless pit of longing. They long for healing, for
wholeness, for comfort, for affirmation, for love; it is in the
nature of human beings that we can only satisfy these needs for
a few hours, perhaps a day, and then we must return with more
comfort, more assurance, more love. Truly we must repeat ourselves and must go round and round in circles of loving until we
are dizzy and exhausted.

Perhaps it is in this endless circular dance of loving that we
begin to learn humility, for the more we love the more we see
how far we fall short of people's needs. Paradoxically it is our
very success that reveals to us the extent of our failure. The
human heart is ever hungry, and we have pitifully little to meet
its needs. But the great joke is that if we are foolish enough to
attempt to feed the five thousand we will learn the truth of the
saying, "Love is like a basket of loaves and fishes: you never

have enough until you start to give it away."

But it takes a lifetime to learn that sort of wisdom, and most of the time we find ourselves holding back for fear that we do not have the resources to meet a particular need. Like the wretched Levite, we find ourselves averting our eyes and hurrying by on the other side of the road. It happened to me not very long ago.

I had gone to London in the hope of negotiating a grant from the Cancer Research Campaign to fund a clinical psychologist who would teach counseling and communication skills. My vision was that we would be able to improve the care of the dying in our local hospitals if nurses and junior doctors were trained how to break bad news and generally cope better with distressed patients and their families. As always I was a little late and I hurried down Picadilly on my way to the CRC offices. As I jostled my way through the crowd I noticed a man lying on the pavement. I stopped about twenty yards away and looked. He seemed to be alive and there was no sign of hemorrhage. Standing above him was a very young and embarrassed security guard from one of the big stores, clutching a walkie-talkie in his hand and obviously waiting for assistance. The people passed by, apparently oblivious. I stood my ground. Should I go up and declare myself a doctor? Should I go and kneel down by the man and ask him what was wrong—try to comfort him? I felt I should do both these things—but I did neither. I felt a great distaste for being involved medically in that situation at that precise moment. It would make me late for my meeting; I might be expected to go to the hospital with him in an ambulance. Maybe he would suddenly stop breathing and I would have to struggle with trying cardiac massage and mouth-to-mouth respiration. Eventually I convinced myself that the security guard had everything in hand and went on my way. After about five minutes I came to Leicester Square and realized that I had been walking in the wrong direction. Crossly, I retraced my steps only to find that the man was *still* there. I stopped again. He seemed to be in good color. Someone had put a blanket over him. The security guard still towered over the sad prone figure crumpled under a makeshift blanket. Then as I wrestled with my conscience, an ambulance screamed around the corner and I felt free to escape. I walked away feeling really dirty—and in many ways I still do. I do not propose to make any excuses or even search for explanations: I think the story can stand alone as a sort of anti-parable—an example of the frailty of human beings, of how a professional Samaritan can suddenly find that he or she is, for today, behaving like a Levite. Brooding about it, I found myself a little comforted when I remembered a passage from the American poet Christopher William Jones's *Listen Pilgrim*. Jones, now an Episcopalian monk, uses a vivid prose poetry to drive home the devastating message of Matthew 25:45, "insofar as you neglected to do this to one of the least of these, you neglected to do it to me." Here we meet him at his visionary best devastated by the awareness of Christ in the gutters of New York:

Coming out of Memorial Church one day,
in Greenwich Village on Washington Square in New
York,
I saw a bum
standing in the middle of the street.
Four or five men, two or three women,
all dressed very properly, some with
important looking attaché cases,
passed him, pretending they did not see him,
bumping into him,
pushing aside his stretched hand;
and I followed them.
And I still think that
for me
this was sin,
because there was this Lord and God
of mine and yours,
dirty,
smelling
like the lavatory in which he slept
that night,
filthy, despairing, drunk,
and demanding—not humbly asking, but demanding—

money.

Who was he to demand?

Christopher William Jones
Listen Pilgrim

The more I try to write about caring, the more I find myself
in a state of interior muddle and conflict. I know how I *should*
be acting—and yet I do not always do it! Like St. Paul, I want
to howl: "I cannot understand my own behavior, I fail to carry
out the things I want to do, and I find myself doing the very
things I hate" (Rom. 7:15).

"What am I?" I ask myself, "Samaritan or Levite?" At first
sight it is always so easy to identify the goodies and the baddies.
In my world the goodies are the gentle, loving, compassionate
doctors and nurses who, when asked to come and see someone
out of hours, say, "Of course, no problem, I'll be around as soon
as I can"—and the baddies are those who will not come, or if
they do come are surly or pompous or unfriendly. And yet I find
myself all too frequently playing both parts: goodie on the bright
sunny days when I have slept well or am not too hassled; but
baddie on the other, too frequent, dark days when I am tired
and overburdened and desperately in need of a little time out.
There seems an appalling gulf between what I preach and what
I practice, a massive shortfall on Jesus' counsel of perfection:
"You must love the Lord your God with all your heart, with all
your soul, with all your strength, and with all your mind, and
your neighbor as yourself" (Luke 10:27). This, of course, "the
greatest commandment," is a summary of the Law and the
Prophets. The first injunction regarding worship comes from
Deuteronomy: "Listen, Israel: Yahweh our God is the one Yahweh. You shall love Yahweh your God with all your heart, with
all your soul, with all your strength. Let these words I urge on
you today be written on your heart" (Deut. 6:4-6).

This verse which forms the words of the Shema, a prayer still
central to Jewish worship, gives us the key to the possibility of
the second half of the commandment: "You must love your
neighbor as yourself." This second part of the quotation comes
from a passage in Leviticus where Yahweh provides a detailed
moral code for the children of Israel, telling them, when you

gather the harvest of your land, do not strip the fields bare. Leave a little at the edges so that when you have gone home with your crop and the poor come creeping in at dusk, there is something left over for them. And when you harvest your grapes, leave a few bunches on the vine. Do not be too eager to gather up the fallen fruit. You do not really need it, so why not leave it for those who do, for those who have no money to buy food from the shops and for the weary traveler, parched with the dust of the road. Do not be mean or greedy, over-protective of your own rights. More than anything, do not be a dog in the manger, destroying what you do not need. You must leave them for the poor and the stranger. I am Yahweh your God.

It is not just the farmers who get told how to behave; the law of the Lord extends into the heart of the city. Employers must be fair and just and take care of their workers, not hanging onto their wages until the last possible minute; and businessmen must be honest in their affairs. Insider trading is definitely out and judges must be impartial in their rulings. No area of life is overlooked and the call to justice is unequivocal. But the law does not end at justice, an eye for an eye, a tooth for a tooth. We must not hate, even when there is good reason, or we take the other's sin upon ourselves. When we have been wronged we must take no vengeance, but forgive. To put it in a nutshell, God says: "You must love your neighbor as yourself. I am Yahweh." Of course, it is that last phrase that is so hard to swallow and to live out: the loving of neighbor as self. The lawyer in Luke 10 tried to catch Jesus by asking him "and who is my neighbor?" but Jesus' parable of the Good Samaritan showed him clearly that there can be no boundaries to loving, that the person needing love at that particular moment was an outsider and it was in fact an outsider who took compassion on him. He who was neighbor to the injured man was the man on the spot who, without thought for his own convenience and safety, perceived a need and acted on it with the resources available to him. He did not say, as he might legitimately have done, "I am too busy; maybe he is faking and will jump on me; it's no good my stopping because I would not know what to do; the ambulance will be along in a minute." No. He stopped and did what he could. And we are bade to go and do the same.

The lesson for me and for all of us about stopping to attend to the injured in our path is an obvious one — though as my own sad little experience shows, it is all too easy to be a Levite. How are we twentieth-century Christians to take this story? Am I being absurdly fundamentalist in dwelling upon it like this? Or is this commandment indeed pivotal in our discipleship; should we professional carers be struggling to love our patients as ourselves? In recent years I have, from time to time, been cast in the role of patient rather than doctor and the experience has been salutary. It has made me acutely aware of how the medical system, of which I am a part, can unconsciously hurt those it sets out to heal.

As in all the areas of caring which I have explored, there is need for an understanding of both points of view, a tempering of criticism with compassion. A couple of years ago I attended a gynecological clinic. As is the custom, I was asked to undress and don a hospital dressing gown. Thus decently clad, but divested of most of my dignity, I was ushered into the clinic. The doctor pleasantly bade me sit down and asked what the trouble was. Frozen to my chair, I looked at him and then at the nurse who stood beside him. She turned her back on me and began to busy herself with some papers as if to say, "don't mind me." But I *did* mind her — most dreadfully. The idea of having to discuss my symptoms with the doctor was bad enough, but that there should be a third party listening-in was too much. I felt horribly humiliated and muttered that I could not talk in front of the nurse. The doctor feigned not to hear or understand and I stumbled on as best I could. Now, as it happens, my problems were not particularly embarrassing and I am not unduly shy; I just found it awful to have no privacy, and even more awful to be made to feel a fool because I was making a fuss.

It was this experience that first set me thinking about the way we professionals handle people in outpatient clinics. Nearly all patients who come to hospital clinics experience a degree of anxiety. They are worried about being unwell, anxious about what will be found and concerned that they will irritate the doctor who is so clever and so busy. They fear too that they will look a fool because they cannot explain themselves clearly. In most clinics, however, instead of helping people to feel at ease, we divest them of their carefully chosen clothes, thereby reducing their sense of being a "proper person." Then, when we have rendered them even more vulnerable, we expect them to discuss their intimate problems and expose their bodies in the presence of strangers. And if then they exhibit their anxiety we write them off as being neurotic! Perhaps all nurses and doctors should "role play" being a patient every couple of years. They should learn what it feels like to be wheeled down the corridor on a stretcher in a paper hat, to have the various "routine" investigations; they should know that having blood tests is sometimes very painful, and that having metal instruments inserted into various bodily orifices can be very unpleasant indeed. More than anything, they should remember how horrid it is to feel foolish or misunderstood and that the fear of being thought neurotic is often worse than the finding of a genuine pathology!

If I am outspoken in my criticism of the way doctors and nurses handle patients, it must be remembered that I speak from the inside, and that I am often as guilty as my colleagues of causing distress; I, like them, am caught up in a complex pattern of behavior which is conditioned by years of tradition and a very genuine shortage of human and material resources. One of my colleagues sees fifty women with breast cancer in a single clinic. Even with two or three doctors helping him, it is impossible that he should see each patient fully clothed. It is likewise impossible that he should ask her how she feels about the disease, how her husband is reacting to her mutilation, how she feels in her spirits. It is no wonder that recent research shows that many cases of severe anxiety, depression, and psychological disturbance are being missed in women with breast cancer. The doctors are so busy attending to the physical side of their patient's disease that they pay scant attention to the psychological issues. As one gynecologist said to me recently about sexual dysfunction: "That's a whole Pandora's box I'd rather not open."

Sick people are not called "patients" for nothing. It is as well for us carers that they will put up with endless pain and indignity and still be grateful to us for doing our best. Again and again it comes home to me that we professionals are a frail and wounded race; like G. K. Chesterton in his *Hymn for the Church Militant,* we can sing:

Great God, that bowest sky and star,
Bow down our towering thoughts to thee,
And grant us in a faltering war
The firm feet of humility.

Lord, we that snatch the swords of flame,
Lord, we that cry about thy ear,
We too are weak with pride and shame,
We too are as our foe-man are.

Yea we are mad as they are mad,
Yea we are blind as they are blind,
Yea we are very sick and sad
Who bring good news to all mankind.

⊰{ 6 }⊱

HOLY THURSDAY

When he had washed their feet and put on his clothes again Jesus went back to the table. "Do you understand," he said, "what I have done to you? You call me Master and Lord, and rightly; so I am. If I, then, the Lord and Master, have washed your feet, you should wash each other's feet. I have given you an example so that you may copy what I have done to you." (John 13:12-15)

I spent Easter at L'Arche, a community of handicapped people and their helpers, which lies in the French village of Trosly Breuil on the edge of the forest outside Compiegne. The community, which began in 1964 with two handicapped men and a gentle French Canadian named Jean Vanier, is now home to two hundred men and women, handicapped and helpers, who live together in *foyers,* ordinary houses, in groups of anything from ten to twenty. As an outsider with little French I often find it difficult to distinguish between carers and handicapped, for the boundaries are frequently blurred. Perhaps the most important thing that L'Arche has taught me is that labels are of little consequence, for we are all wounded, handicapped in some way or another. Having long feared to come to L'Arche because I thought I could not cope with the mentally handicapped, I find myself absurdly at home, recognizing for the first time that I too am handicapped, hurt and maimed from birth and by circumstance and that this is an acceptable way of being a person.

On Holy Thursday we celebrated the liturgy of the institution of the Eucharist and washing of the feet. I have a deep love of these Holy Week services and for many years have spent the Easter Triduum at Ampleforth, a Benedictine monastery in the North of England where the monks open their doors to share their prayer with a large number of lay people like me. On Holy Thursday night the abbot and a number of other priests celebrate Mass and as a part of the liturgy they wash the feet of twelve men from the congregation. This washing is a rather stylized affair, with the abbot, girded in a towel, pouring water from a silver jug on a clean pink foot held over a large silver bowl. It is a symbolic act, a ritualized re-enactment of an old story: that Jesus, the night before he was betrayed, rose from the supper table, tied a towel around his waist and washed the feet of his disciples. When he had finished he returned to the table and asked his disciples, "Do you understand what I have done to you?" One can imagine them looking blankly at him and then at each other. What on earth was he doing, he, their rabbi and master, humbling himself to touch their dirty feet, caked in the dust of the Palestine roads? How did he speak to them, I wonder? Gently, or with an undertone of urgency and mild exasperation? This was his last time with them, his last chance to instill in them the principles of a way of living so different from the norm that they still could not grasp it. "Look," he said, "you call me Master and Lord, and rightly, for that's what I am. So if I, your Lord and Master, have washed *your* feet, so *you* should wash one another's feet. Do you see? I have given you an example so that you can copy what I have done to you."

That night in L'Arche, in the *foyer* they call Le Val Fleury, I witnessed a re-enactment of this scene that left me spellbound and gave me new insights into Jesus' last, most urgent commandment — that we must love one another just as he had loved us. The evening went on like this: at first we all gathered for Mass, a glorious motley of several hundred people, men, women and children, the handicapped and the outwardly whole, in a large meeting room. There were readings, hymns and a flute solo, woven into the celebration of the Eucharist, the memorial of Jesus' last supper with his friends. As always at L'Arche the service was long but everyone seemed happy, even toddlers who roamed freely around the church as whim and courage took them. Then came the supper in our *foyer* with forty to fifty people gathered around a long table. There were Luisa from Italy, two Marias from Austria, and a professor of geophysics from Paris who had been born in Vietnam. There was Jean, who began it all, gentle, shabby and full of laughter, and Barbara, his assistant, tiny with shining eyes and mind and wit razor sharp, flitting from language to language as she spoke to the people around her. My neighbor Ted was from Toronto, a Jesuit student studying theology in Paris, drawn, like myself, by the magic of this unwieldy family.

After the meal Jean spoke a little of the meaning behind our celebration: of Abraham, the first Jew, who had taken his family into an unknown land, a prototype of all who find themselves answering a call into the unknown; and of Moses who led the people of Israel from the slavery of Egypt into the Promised Land. God loved the people of Israel so much that he rescued them and they, in their turn, were to remember their liberation by celebrating the Passover meal; by remembering the story and telling it to their children. And now we were remembering another Passover meal—the last one that Jesus shared with his disciples before he gave himself up for them. Greater love hath no person, man or woman, than to give themselves for the love of another. This is the magic and mystery of our humanity that one man will sacrifice himself for another, in the gift of a life spent in service or in one incredible gesture of love, like that of Maximilian Kolbe, the Polish priest who took the place of a condemned man in the death chambers of Auschwitz. Individually and together we recalled the gifts of the past year. It was hard for me to understand the muttered words of the native French speakers, but now and again I caught the more stilted phrases of foreigners like myself, for whom the gift of the love in L'Arche had brought a new dimension to their lives. The halting words of the carers, trying to express what God had meant to them this year, were balanced by the simplicity of the handicapped for whom a gift or trip had been a precious sign that they were loved.

When all had had their turn to speak we moved to another room and arranged ourselves in a great circle for the washing of the feet. A carer and a handicapped man sat in the center of the group, waiting with towel and basin for the ceremony to begin. Then it was the turn of Xavier, the professor from Paris, to speak. Had we noticed, he asked, that St. John had omitted the passage of the Eucharist from his account of the Last Supper? The other gospels related how Jesus had taken bread and broken it and given it to his disciples, telling them that this was his body, given for them. But not John. Instead he told how Jesus had taken a bowl of water and a towel and washed his disciples' feet. He had replaced one story with another. Why? Because they conveyed the same message: that life was about sacrifice, about service, and the love of God must be paid out in love of neighbor. Greater love hath no man than he who pours out his life for another. And life is not just blood given once and for all, it is time and energy, tears and laughter, poured out hourly, daily, over a lifetime.

Impatiently, Michel waited, poised to wash the feet of Patrick, the man seated in front of him. I'm not sure how much he understood of what the professor said. His eyes were fixed on the water and he held the towel in readiness. At last he was allowed to begin. No silver jug and basin here, and certainly no symbolic or ritual ablution! This was the real thing: a washing up bowl, full of warm soapy water with Patrick's foot plunged firmly in. Lovingly, Michel soaped it, up and down, round the heel and then gently between each toe. At last, he was satisfied, and lifted it out onto his lap to dry. Gently he patted the clean skin and separated the toes, drying each one individually. Then the other foot was soaped, rinsed and dried with equal care. I sat fascinated. Here was the carer being tended by his charge. Here was Michel, the simpleton, showing us how to love. It was not just the gentleness, but the rapt concentration and attention to detail. He was showing us in his own way that people are precious, that the human body is wondrously beautiful, to be honored and handled with care. I was reminded of times I had seen nurses at the hospice, washing an unconscious patient with such infinite tenderness that it breaks my heart. This manner of handling the body is for some an instinctive thing, an expression of a love that possesses the carer, driving out natural squeamishness or distaste and replacing it with an innate sense of the holiness of people, of their infinite worth.

I find in this unselfconscious love a very special revelation of God. It struck me the first time I visited L'Arche and sat up in the gallery at Mass watching the helpers with their charges. The natural tenderness with which they handled the profoundly handicapped touched me deeply. There was something so moving in the contact between the youth and beauty of these carers and the deformed bodies and damaged intellects of their charges. They sat together on a rug at the foot of the altar, arms entwined, stroking the hair and whispering gently in the ear of the person they were holding. I thought of the majority of the profoundly handicapped, hidden in the wards of long-stay hospitals and of the way they are shunned by those of us who are strong and whole. Their very existence poses questions about God and life and human values that we find difficult to answer. And here were these young helpers, so beautiful and full of promise spending their love and vitality upon these broken creatures, with their necks awry, their eyes rolling and their tongues monstrously protruding from their open mouths. As I watched, I remembered anew this fragment of Sidney Carter's poem, which speaks so powerfully of my own work:

> Over this dead loss to society
> you pour your precious ointment.
> You wash the feet
> that will not walk tomorrow.
> Call the bluff and laugh
> at the fat and clock-faced gravity
> of our economy.

I have a deep sense of the wholeness of the liturgy at L'Arche—a liturgy in which everyone has their place. The presence of the handicapped at the foot of the altar is somehow so right and fitting. They are there at the heart of the liturgy, given pride of place at the table. It is difficult to write without sounding sentimental—perhaps I am—but I find myself so much more at home here, with this motley of people and little children wandering about, than I do at my own parish church. There is a deep sense of reverence in the congregation that has nothing to do with arriving on time or kneeling up straight in a pew. Mothers with tiny babies wander in and out, clumsy handicapped men lurch unselfconsciously to their feet and go out for awhile and then return, physically disturbing their neighbors, yet somehow not breaking the silence. Many of the less severely handicapped act as acolytes and they too merge into the liturgy. There is a sense of acceptance of all that makes each person comfortable and therefore not disturbed by behavior which would be unbearably intrusive in another environment. Truly, this is for me, as Eliot would say, a place where worship is valid.

> You are not here to verify,
> Instruct yourself, or inform curiosity
> Or carry report. You are here to kneel
> Where prayer has been valid. And prayer is more
> Than an order of words, the conscious occupation
> Of the praying mind, or the sound of the voice
> praying.
>
> T. S. Eliot, *Little Gidding*

Our foot-washing liturgy took over an hour, but rarely have I been so prayerful and at home among strangers. Each person washed the feet of his or her neighbor; when the water got a bit grey and the towel sodden, a fresh bowl and a dry towel were brought. It was a joy to watch the handicapped for they brought simplicity and seriousness to an act which otherwise might have been banal. From time to time there was laughter which flowed as naturally in the silence as the babies gurgling in church. It was a good time to watch, to pray and to reflect. At one stage in the proceedings I had a strange sense of the beauty of these people. It was not that they were pretty or that they glowed or were illuminated, I just *saw* them as beautiful—not different. They just *looked* beautiful to me, their faces full of concentration, gentleness and laughter. I felt as though I were seeing them through God's eyes, and knew briefly how it was that God loves them—each one so different and so precious.

I am conscious that I write rather emotionally about a group of ordinary people who live, love and hate just as the rest of us do.

I believe, however, that sometimes one is given a glimpse of a deeper truth about life and people—an eternal truth which lies beyond the immediate. It is not so much that the handicapped and their helpers are special and holy but that their way of life makes the uniqueness and holiness which is innate in humans easier for me to see. I know well that the hospice where I work provides the same experience of revelation for many people. Most of the time I am so close to it that I am blind to the power of what we are doing: a foot-washing of a different sort.

I remember well the night I was given the Sidney Carter poem that I quoted earlier:

No revolution will come in time
to alter this man's life
except the one surprise
of being loved.

I had been asked to speak to a group of volunteers from the Home Care service in a nearby town. I was so exhausted by pressures of work and a heavy schedule of lectures that I could not face the hour's drive and asked my secretary to take me. We had been invited to supper by the woman involved with the volunteers, and as we sat at the table her husband asked me if I had been "healed" of my experience in prison. Finding the question bewildering and intrusive, I muttered something a bit sharp in reply whereupon his wife asked me brightly what had been my worst experience in prison! My secretary, sensing that I was about to explode, either in tears or rage, managed to avert the conversation so there was no ugly scene. Later in the evening when the talk was over my hostess gave me a copy of the poem— a passage which has given me greater theological insight into my work than anything else I have seen written.

The next day one of my patients, Frank, a lovely North countryman suddenly went off his legs—became paralyzed from the waist down because the cancer in his kidney had invaded his spine. Over the next few days we explained to him that he would not walk again, and tried to help him grapple with the terrifying loss of his strength, independence and privacy. As I drove around the city and walked down the hospital corridors, I found myself saying again and again, "You wash the feet that will not walk tomorrow," and realized that this was *my* job, my calling. I, who have little patience with the demented and no love for tiny babies, have a special gift of warmth and understanding for those whose time is running out. I, who hate parties and find it nigh impossible to make small talk, know instinctively what to say and do for a gentle Manchester builder who is facing the humiliation of incontinence and the fear of death.

For everything, there is a season, for every task, someone is given the tools.

⋖ 7 ⋗

Precious Spikenard

And then took Mary a pound of ointment of Spikenard very costly, and anointed the feet of Jesus, and wiped his feet with her hair. (John 12:3)

The next day was Good Friday and as I sat at the breakfast table in the guest house at L'Arche there was the usual kaleidoscope of people from all over the world, passing through this strange crossroads for a day, a weekend or perhaps a year. Over coffee and French bread one meets professors and tramps, nuns and dentists, missionaries and an endless variety of young people from Sweden, Japan, England — it seems from every nation under heaven. That morning's brief encounter was with Claudette, a French Canadian from Montreal; Alexandra, a French university student; and Jonathan, a young Irishman working in a house for down-and-outs in Paris. He had a particular vitality and charm, laughing and clowning in the sunshine of the spring morning and I thought to myself, here it is again, that razor-edged sign of God in our times: the young pouring their lives out in lavish abandon on the useless members of society. What on earth, I thought, is this young Irishman doing working with tramps in Paris? What, one might equally ask, is a twenty-two-year-old Irish girl I know doing working in the latest L'Arche foundation in Bethany, near Jerusalem? She wrote to me the other day, sitting on the bathroom floor waiting for a handicapped Arab woman to move her bowels. What, in God's name is Gaby doing there?

That's it, of course; she is there in God's name. That is the only way to make sense of it. It is a particular form of Christian madness that seeks out the broken ones, the insane, the handicapped and the dying and places before their astonished eyes a banquet normally reserved for the whole and the productive. One could, of course, look for all manner of psychological motives behind this kind of giving. These young people are perhaps rebelling against over-protective parents, or searching desperately for a love they were denied by mothers who had themselves been damaged somewhere along the way. Like the doctors and the nurses, priests and social workers, they number among the ranks of Chesterton's "sick and sad, who bring good news to all mankind." Oh, of course we are all sick and sad, wounded somewhere in the heart or psyche. Perhaps we are all sublimating some great sexual drive or yearning for parental love. But the *facts* are that the blind see, the lame walk and the poor have the good news preached to them, and where these things are happening we find the kingdom: God is somehow revealed as present among his people.

It has taken me a long time to understand this. At first I saw my own acts of service and those of others as out of the ordinary — special and holy. Then, as I explored my motives and drives, I realized that much of what I had interpreted as a direct call from God, his hand in my life, could equally well be explained in psychological terms: the result of childhood experiences and relations with my parents. I saw that my great religious calling was, in fact, a product of childhood repression and yearning for love and affirmation. At first this insight was enormously painful and for a while I was moved to reject all the religious structures and language that had so long upheld me. Then after a few months I rediscovered my faith at a different, perhaps deeper level. I found that the knowledge of the workings of my emotions and unconscious was totally compatible with belief in God and the theories of call and covenant with which I had been raised. Perhaps it was analogous to the move one makes from the childhood fundamentalist understanding of the creation story to the synthesis of evolution theories and belief in an all-powerful creator God. At first one finds the mat withdrawn sharply from under one's feet and all props removed, but after a while one learns to live with mystery and unknowing. I can now accept that I am driven by my unconscious—but I see my wounded psyche as somehow part of *my* story which in its turn is part of the salvation history of all those whose lives I touch.

Touch. Perhaps that is the key word to understanding the way God works. Over the years my life has been touched by so many different men and women. There was Sister Mary Teresa, the chemistry teacher on whom I had a schoolgirl crush and who influenced me to feel called to be a nun. A by-product of this first flowering of childhood love was the fact that to please her I drove myself to learn five years of chemistry in two, and so got a place at university that I might otherwise never have managed! And so it has been over the years. A succession of heroes and falling-in-love have led me from a comfortable middle-class family with no overt social conscience into the world of missionaries and martyrs, hospices and homes for the handicapped.

Perhaps if I had not been hurt as a child, I would now be happily married with sons and daughters at university or art school. But no—for various reasons I find myself alone, at home on the margins of the professional world and the institutional church, pouring my precious ointment over those who, in economic terms, are quite useless.

I find in the story of the anointing at Bethany a marvelous image of the work of hospices or communities like L'Arche. The story goes that Jesus was at a dinner party in the house of one Simon the leper. It was six days before the Passover and he was in hiding from those who were out to get him. As they sat at the table a woman came in with a box of precious ointment. The King James Bible speaks of an alabaster jar of precious spikenard, a fragrant ointment used to anoint the bodies of the dead. All the Gospel accounts stress that it could have been sold for three hundred denarii—nearly a year's wages or the price of a car. And yet this foolish woman came in and broke the jar and poured it over Jesus' feet. What on earth did she think she was doing—making a spectacle of herself and Jesus, wasting money in a lavish public expression of love? As the scent of the ointment filled the house the people muttered, "How dare she; that stuff could have been sold and the money given to the poor." But Jesus told them not to upset her, that the story of her outrageous gesture of love would be told whenever his story was related for future generations.

I find it fascinating to speculate what was behind this act. John tells us that the woman was in fact Martha's sister Mary, the woman who had sat adoringly at his feet as he preached. It is clear from the story of the raising of Lazarus from the dead that Mary of Bethany and Jesus were close friends—perhaps she was even the Mary of Magdala, from whom he had "cast out seven devils." Be that as it may, one can imagine that Mary knew what was on Jesus' mind—that he was sad and afraid as the days of confrontation approach. He knew quite well that he would be arrested and killed and yet he was driven to go forward when he might well have run away. Perhaps he sat at that party making polite conversation or carrying on with his teaching work—but inwardly sick and afraid of what was to come. Mary's extravagant gesture must have been her way of saying to him, "I love you. I know what is going on inside you. I can't stop it happening, but I want you to know that I care and to take the memory of my love with you, to comfort you in the dark days ahead." Perhaps this episode gave Jesus the strength he needed, at that moment, to carry on with his mission.

In the same way the love that we pour out on the dying or the handicapped says many things. It is an expression of *our* need to serve, to love, however flawed our motives. To the person cared for it is the gesture that makes the pain bearable, life somehow worth living:

> No revolution will come in time
> to alter this man's life
> except the one surprise
> of being loved.
>   Sidney Carter

But the most important message is the unspoken one to the world at large: that this "dead loss to society," this dying woman or handicapped man, is infinitely precious. If I as a doctor spend an hour of my clinic time talking to a woman who has only a few weeks to live, I am making a clear statement of her worth. I am giving her time that could have been spent with people who will get better, who will be able to contribute once again to the common good. I am affirming the worth of one individual person in a world in which the individual is at risk of being submerged or valued only for his strength, intellect or beauty. It is a prophetic statement about the unique value of the human person, irrespective of age, social class, or productivity. It is an affirmation that people matter just *because they are people,* because God made them and loves them, just as they are, not because they are good or witty or physically beautiful.

It seems to me that hospices and places like L'Arche have unconsciously taken on a prophetic role in the church and in society at large. They evangelize in the most effective way — unconsciously — by living a faith that is credible to unbelievers. I saw this clearly in Chile, where the institutionalized church which had become identified with the landowners had long since lost credibility with the ordinary people, especially the young. It was only when church people left the security of their institutions and risked comfort, health and even life for the poor and the oppressed that they proclaimed the gospel in a language that could be understood. Of course the great paradox is that those who make a radical option for the poor often become a threat to their fellow Christians. This is particularly the case where there is a massive gulf between the rich and the poor. The poor are inevitably a threat to the rich, either because they make them feel guilty or because they think that they will try to take away their possessions. It is the same with the handicapped and the dying. We isolate the handicapped on the pretext that they will disturb the peace — when the reality is that their presence disturbs our desire for the beautiful. We isolate our dying on the pretext that they want peace — when the reality is that their presence disturbs our sense of omnipotence and immortality.

When Christians make radical options for the economically poor they enter into solidarity with them. They see the world and economic structures through their eyes: that is, they become aware of a society in which ten per cent of the people own ninety per cent of the resources of a world in which a small group of people eat their fill of fine food and drink while the rest starve. When I first went to Chile I made friends with the people from the Embassy and from the rich landowner classes. I enjoyed their company, their houses and their cuisine, but later on, when I became captive to the warmth and laughter of the missionaries living in the shanty towns, I was no longer at ease in the old dispensation. I could no longer make light conversation at the dinner parties of the rich and I ceased to be welcome at their table. It is so easy for those who work with the poor to be labeled Marxists when their allegiance is to the stripped bones of the Christian gospel. It is more comfortable for the members of a wealthy church to believe that their brothers and sisters have been corrupted than that they have seen the light of Christ.

In a much lesser way, those who opt to work with the physically dispossessed have become uncomfortable colleagues. I become tiresome when I spend an hour on one patient in a clinic which is used to processing someone every ten minutes. My treatment takes longer so it is more expensive. It also costs more in emotional resources and is more threatening, because if I ask the dying how they *feel* about their illness and their treatment I am liable to expose their anger at having their diagnosis missed or at having treatment that has prolonged their life at the expense of destroying its quality. Even if all has gone as smoothly as possible, those who become close to the dying become a sign of the ultimate impotence of technology and medicine. Hospices are in a curious way a sign of the failure of medicine to conquer disease: they force us to admit that there are limits to our powers of healing.

L'Arche too poses a threat to a society which locks its handicapped in institutions. When I see the fullness of life that can be lived by these people, I weep that it cannot be given to all — that this movement is but a drop in the ocean. And it cannot be given to all because the resources, human and economic, are not thus allocated. And the resources are not allocated because as a society we place our values elsewhere: upon raising the standard of living of a minority and then defending that way of life to such an extent that there are not enough resources to provide adequate housing and medical care and education for all.

The option for the radical gospel is always divisive — as Jesus was divisive — because it threatens to fill the hungry with good things and send the rich away empty.

Meanwhile there will always be those who find themselves called like Mary at Bethany to disturb the peace by pouring out over some dead loss to society that which could have been sold for three hundred denarii.

⊰ 8 ⊱

STABAT MATER

Near the cross of Jesus stood his mother and his mother's sister, Mary the wife of Clopas, and Mary of Magdala. (John 19:25)

Stabat mater Dolorosa
Juxta crucem lacrimosa
Dum pendebat filius.

Cujus animam gementem
Contristatem et dolentum
Per transivit gladius.

At the cross her station keeping
Stood the mournful mother weeping
Close to Jesus to the last.

Through her soul of joy bereaved
Bowed in anguish deeply grieved
Now at length the sword had passed.

Jacobo Benedetti
from *Stabat Mater*
Fourteenth-century hymn for the
feast of Our Lady of Sorrows

In the care of the dying, as in many other fields of endeavor, there comes a time when the carer's hands are empty, when all the treatment maneuvers have been explored, all the words of comfort said. It is then that one is left standing at the foot of the bed, useless, impotent, wanting more than anything else to run away.

The first lines of *Stabat Mater,* etched in my memory from twenty years of pre-Vatican II liturgies, capture better than any photograph the agony of the death-bed vigil. In seven years of caring for the dying, I have stood at over a thousand bedsides and shared in the impotence of families and friends as they watched the life ebb away from someone they love. This powerlessness to prevent impending death is one of the hardest things for carers to come to terms with, especially when the dying person is young. It produces all sorts of emotions which are often unexpected and hard to handle and may lead to patterns of behavior which, misunderstood, can cause considerable distress, both to the person experiencing the emotion and those around him. The hospice movement, with its philosophy of openness, is producing a marvelous healing of the medical and nursing profession's wounded attitude towards death and dying, a recapturing of the ancient acceptance of death as part of life.

It is here that we must learn the spirituality of the foot of the cross, the stance of the impotent bystander. Of all the vigils that come to mind the one that I recall with greatest heartache is that of a young woman called Ros who died in our hospice on Christmas day. Ros was only twenty-eight when she died. She had a brain tumor which recurred a year after treatment and, in its final stages, caused her terrible headaches and bizarre hallucinations. Her last days at the hospice have remained fresh in my memory because of the singular poignancy of the circumstances. Ros was a doctor and, knowing that the tumor had recurred, faced death with a particular courage and charm. Absurdly, of course, she thought she was a coward — as the brave always do. She mistook fear for cowardice, and wept for her frailty, angry that she was not coping as well as she had hoped. At a loss to know what to say, I remembered the preface of Martyrs, copied it out and gave it to her, shyly, because what helps one person may be useless to another:

Her death reveals your power
shining through our human weakness.

You choose the weak and make them strong
in bearing witness to you . . .

I like to think it helped. Anyway, she gathered strength and
went home for a week, and then when things became bad came
back. Together we faced the last lap. As it happens it was the
week before Christmas, and Ros's mother kept vigil at her
bedside amid the decoration of the house and all the prepa-
rations for the coming feast. Ros was unconscious now, her
pale face tranquil and her dark hair, lovingly brushed by the
nurses, silhouetted against the pillow. Fit young people with
brain tumors often take a long time to die and Ros was no
exception. It must have been three or four days, perhaps
longer, that her mother sat — a quiet composed woman, apparently asking nothing more of us than we gave her by instinct
and by profession. Surely, I thought, this is the stuff of Holy
Week, not Christmas, of the woman at the foot of the cross,
not the Madonna.

When a dying person is unconscious the carers' focus shifts
instinctively to whoever is the principal mourner. They must
be cherished, accompanied, supported, in whatever way seems
right for them. There is no blueprint for the care of the grieving — some wish to keep constant vigil, sitting or sleeping at
the bedside until the moment of death and beyond. Others
find themselves unbearably distressed or even revolted and
need permission to go home. More than anything they need
to know that, however they feel, that is O.K. If they want to
stay they will not be a burden, and if they cannot bear to come
in, we will not think badly of them. We give this kind of support instinctively now, but from time to time we too fall into
the trap of judging people as being selfish or uncaring when
really they are possessed by a grief too great to bear. It can
be particularly difficult when families are divided among
themselves; for instance, when parents, divorced and remar-
ried, come together again at the bedside of an only child.
Sometimes there is real unpleasantness as people fight for the
right to be at the bedside and we have to be very firm in order
to protect the child from the burden of jealousy and posses-
siveness.

Another very difficult scenario is the conflict between a young wife or husband and the parents of their dying spouse. It happens commonly when a young wife is dying and her husband has to cope with looking after the children while holding down his job. The girl's mother, distraught at the loss of her daughter, is often blind to the need of the husband and wife to be alone together. Sometimes the hospice provides a sort of neutral ground in which all those grieving can find space to be with the person who is dying without usurping the role of the other.

And in the midst of all this grief and tension, what of the professional carers? What do they feel? It has long been assumed in medical nursing circles that it is wrong for the carers to become "involved" and I have struggled with this issue in Chapter 3. The fact remains that, however professionally correct they are, carers are inevitably caught up in the tragedy of untimely death. One of the key factors in my experience is to identify with the patient or close relatives. Many of the nurses with whom I work are in their mid-forties and they are particularly vulnerable to identification with the young married women who are desolate at leaving their children. I, as a single person, am most vulnerable to the rather off-beat professional people or the very young and find myself taking their pain home with me.

For all of us, however, there is some respite from pain when we can *do* something. In a way the nurses are luckier than the doctors, for there is always *something* they can do: washing, tidying, massaging pressure points. These loving actions somehow soak up the pain. On the other hand, however, the nurses are on the front line, inescapably exposed to the reality of pain and physical and psychic disintegration.

The doctors' burden is a different one. They too are happiest when they can *do* something: adjust medication, drain off fluids, give injections. The hardest thing is to keep on visiting when all the physical maneuvers have been exhausted.

The illustrations that follow are designed to show how many of us cope with ministering to the dying. The first drawing shows the doctor, armed with his competence and his instruments and protected by his aide.

It is the same for the priest performing his sacramental ministry. Here we see him in his stole and collar protected by having a role to play and a ritual to perform.

In the next drawing we see the patient meeting with either doctor or clergyman when he has exhausted the physical aspects of his ministry. He is left with his hands empty—but with his resources of counseling still available.

Much of my work is done like this. I work with my hands physically empty but with a wealth of experience in listening and advising the dying. It is taxing work, for one is always searching for the right word for that particular person. At its best this kind of work is tailored to the needs of the individual. It requires much sensitivity and intuitive skills, for what may be marvelously healing for one person may be disastrously wounding for another. One does not always get it right: I once tried to help a very religious elderly lady by giving her one of our hand crosses—a plain wooden cross which fits into the palm of the hand and can be gripped when someone is afraid or in pain. To my chagrin, she shied violently away from me, repeating desperately, "No, no thank you, I'd rather not." What I had not realized was that this woman was a member of the Plymouth Brethren and objects like the cross were anathema to her.

The last drawing shows both patient and carer stripped of their resources, present to each other, naked and empty-handed, as two human beings.

There is a terrible pain in this impotence, in admitting that one has nothing more to give. It happened to me a little while ago when a young woman lecturer was dying from a slow asphyxiation. Her lungs were filling up with tumor and she sat in her room surrounded by flowers, classical music playing on a tape recorder — and gasping for breath. There are many things one can do for breathlessness, but when the lungs are taken over by tumor there comes a point when there is nothing one can do and people die of lack of oxygen. I sat on the bed with my arm lightly round her heaving shoulders as she asked in despair, "Can't you *do* something?" Gently I said, "I'm sorry — there's nothing I can do." (I could have sedated her, but we had already discussed this and she wanted to remain alert.) She gasped out, "Oh, *don't* say that!" The pain of moments like that is hard to bear. It would have been easier to have said, "Yes, of course," and given her a useless injection or a powerful sedative. Either of these courses would have been professionally correct, but quite wrong for her. Gasping for breath, and blue as she was, she had a magnificent dignity, sitting imperiously with her husband, friends flying in from abroad to bid her farewell. Hers was a death I would be glad to die — a hard bitter agony, but in control to the last.

Slowly, as the years go by, I learn about the importance of powerlessness. I experience it in my own life and I live with it in my work. The secret is not to be afraid of it — not to run away. The dying know we are not God. They accept that we cannot halt the process of cancer, the inexorable march of that terrible army that takes over a human body like an occupying force, pillaging, raping, desecrating without respect and without quarter. All they ask is that we do not desert them: that we stand our ground at the foot of the cross. At this stage of the journey, of being there, of simply being, it is, in many ways, the hardest part.

{ 9 }

WHY ME?

Since I have lost all taste for life,
I will give free rein to my complaints;
I shall let my embittered soul speak out.
I shall say to God, "Do not condemn me,
but tell me the reason for your assault."
                                    Job 10:1-2

One of the effects of the constant exposure to pain and death involved in the care of the dying is that one is forced to grapple not only with the "problem of evil," but with God. I believe that our spiritual attitude to suffering is crucial because it not only determines the way we relate to those for whom we care but our very survival as carers. If our attitude is illogical because of ignorance or a flawed theology, we run the risk of being so overwhelmed by pain that we face burnout. If, however, we are able to maintain a paschal overview, keeping the resurrection in the same perspective as the cross, then our inevitable human sadness will be tempered by the joy we experience in our faith in the loving purposes of God.

The prophet Micah tells us that, not only must we act justly and love tenderly but we must *walk humbly* with God. What does it mean to walk humbly with God? Does it mean genuflecting properly in church? Not swearing? Being respectful to the clergy? Not arguing about contraception and fish on Fridays? If that is what it means then I am guilty of even more arrogance and pride than I had thought, and may the Lord have mercy upon me. No, I see humility more in terms of stance before God, a way of being rather than a code of behavior. For those involved in caring, Micah's counsel of humility makes particular demands. It asks that we bow down before the mystery of suffering, allowing our comforting theological idols to be shattered into a thousand pieces. It teaches us to acknowledge our human frailty with joy and laughter, and to rejoice in, not resent, our need for each other. And lastly, it forces upon us the realization that we must pay more than lip service to our need for God. If our Christianity is to be anything more than a convenient label, we must expose ourselves to the transforming power of God in prayer and in the scriptures.

My own childish conceptions of God were dynamited by the experience of living for a year at a Benedictine monastery, where the monks politely but ruthlessly destroyed many of my idols. It was at Ampleforth that I was introduced to the writing of Annie Dillard, the young American woman who won the 1976 Pulitzer Prize with her enchanting book *Pilgrim at Tinker Creek.* My monastic friends found Dillard fascinating because she grapples with the mystery of God and suffering with a marvelous directness and vitality and in a style that is totally devoid of sentimentality. I have come back to Dillard again and again over the years, partly because I love her use of language but also because she makes more theological sense to me than most people. In the following passage from a later book she engages head-on in the why of suffering:

His disciples asked Christ about a roadside beggar who had been blind from birth. "Who did sin, that man or his parents, that he was born blind?" And Christ, who spat on the ground, made mud of his spittle and clay, plastered the mud over the man's eyes, and gave him sight, answered, "Neither hath this man sinned, nor his parents: but that the works of God should be made manifest in him." Really? If we take this answer to refer to the affliction itself—and not the subsequent cure—as "God's works made manifest," then we have, along with "Not as the world gives do I give unto you," two meager, baffling

answers to one of the few questions worth asking, to wit
"What in the Sam Hill is going on here?" (Annie Dillard,
Holy the Firm)

What is going on here? Why do the good suffer? Does God
deliberately *inflict* suffering, or does God, as is suggested in Job
permit it? Could it really be that God is powerless to prevent it?
Does God suffer *with* us or *in* us or is God some sort of loving
but impotent spectator at the agony of the world? These and
many similar questions are what religious people mean when
they talk of the "problem of evil."

I was brought sharply face to face with these questions during
my time in Chile, but more especially when, in 1980, a friend of
mine was murdered in El Salvador. Ita Ford, an American missionary sister in her early forties was killed by the secret police
along with two other American sisters and a lay missioner called
Jean Donovan. At the funeral of the two Maryknoll sisters Mel-
inda Roper, then head of the congregation, gave the panegyric.
One of the things she said has been enormously helpful in my
understanding of how to cope with my own and other people's
problems about suffering and evil. In her sermon she spoke
about suffering as *problem* and suffering as *mystery*. By suffering
as *problem,* she meant the call to feed the hungry, to protect the
orphan, to care for the sick and to work for justice. Suffering as
mystery, however, concerns the cry which rises from the heart of
those who suffer injustice or misfortune: the inevitable *Why?*
Why me? What have I done to deserve this? This is *the* classic
question about the "problem of evil" — the question which is
always addressed to those who dare to profess any kind of a
faith. How should we answer it? Should we even begin to try?

Whether or not they should, religious people *do* try to answer
these questions, though they come to some very different
answers. I became aware of this a couple of years ago when I
was speaking at a conference on the church's healing ministry
to the dying. I found, to my surprise, that the conference members (doctors, nurses, and clergy) were split into two groups:
those who believed in a concept of cosmic struggle in which the
powers of evil personified in the devil were at war with the
powers of goodness personified in Christ; the other group, in

which I found myself infinitely more at home, believed in a God who, somehow, had this world totally in hand.

I had not realized until I went to that meeting how much a person's God-concept or belief structure influences the way he or she relates to those who suffer. Those who believe that illness is caused by the devil will feel they must lay siege to heaven with their prayers and mobilize all the angels and saints to intercede on their behalf. If they are Catholics they will enlist the help of the Carmelites or other enclosed nuns whose prayers they believe to be more powerful than their own. If they belong to other denominations they may start up a prayer chain, telephoning all their friends and their friends' friends. They may even call in someone with a special gift of healing who will come and lay hands upon the sick person, driving out the evil spirits. When David Watson, a well-known Evangelical minister, was ill two friends in the healing ministry flew in from America to pray over him. In *Fear No Evil,* the story of his illness, Watson describes the visit of his friends:

> After some time of praise and worship, Blaine became aware of the activity of the Holy Spirit and laid hands upon my abdomen. The three of them went on, praying, cursing the cancer in the name of Christ, commanding it to wither, and then they claimed God's healing in my body . . . John Wimber warned me that sometimes, in his experience, a tumor will grow after a time of prayer, until it begins to wither and die.
>
> "It might well be that the next scan or two will reveal cancer in your liver, a cancer that is growing. But I believe that the root of it has now been cut. And soon it will begin to die."

David Watson died of cancer on February 17, 1984, just over a year from diagnosis.

What are we to make of those who claim, like these men, that, through prayer, cancer can be healed? I must admit to being very skeptical over the healing issue. I do not doubt for one moment that God has the power to heal—nor do I discount the gospel miracles, but I believe that God rarely exercises this power in the ordinary run of things. I have no quarrel with those who pray for healing, as long as the people praying leave God and the person prayed for some room for maneuver. The difficulties arise when the person involved in the healing promises a cure, or when those praying become convinced that God is going to work a miracle especially for them.

I had experience of this not long ago when a patient I was treating was pressured to go and see a healer. Apparently the healers concerned had heard about her and rang up some mutual friends saying they felt "called" to heal her. They came and prayed over her and told her that the cancer would go. Luckily the woman herself, who had come to a marvelous degree of acceptance about her illness, was only slightly thrown off balance, but her daughter, a fragile girl who was coping with the situation with great difficulty, became terribly upset.

Another belief with which I have difficulty is that God can heal us if our faith is strong enough. There is undeniably a scriptural basis for this, but it is difficult to reconcile with the fact that so many prayers from people with deep faith are frankly not answered. I become concerned when people are made to feel that their failure to be healed is somehow *their* fault — that their faith is not strong enough or they are somehow blocking the power of God. I find it impossible to believe in a God whose power can be blocked by *anything,* human or demonic.

While on this issue of guilt, we should not forget that there are still people who believe that illness is a punishment for sin. I have never actually met anyone who asserts this, but have been indirectly concerned with two instances. The first was when a patient rang a healer and was told over the telephone that she must be a very wicked woman to have breast cancer — and the second was one of our own volunteers who decided to "counsel" a patient at the hospice, telling her she should mend her ways and set her house in order. I would like to have had the chance of meeting these "healers." The dying can do without that sort of evil corruption of the Christian message.

I find it difficult to understand just what is the theology behind this kind of prayer. Do they believe in a God who is just holding his own in the struggle with evil, or one who has to be placated, persuaded to stay his hand? Do they believe in what some people call the Watchmaker God—a creator who has set the world in motion and then sits as a curious bystander, watching people die in agony or slaughter each other? Most of all, do they believe in a *partisan* God who loves the church-going Christian more than the atheist, the virtuous more than the sinner?

A great breakthrough for me in my understanding of God came as a result of my contact with the church in Latin America. It was there that I became acquainted with the concept of a God who takes special delight in the *anawim*, the marginalized, the little people. If God is partisan, this predilection is surely for the poor, the humanly unlovable and the sinner.

Let us explore how this works out in practice. In the hospice where I work, we have two women dying of cancer. Beth is a good Christian, a pillar of her local church, beloved by everyone. The locker beside her bed is crowded with flowers, the wall covered with cards, and her friends are at her bedside at all hours of the day. It is not surprising, for she is truly a lovely woman, brave and charming, radiating joy to all of us. And in the other bed is Mary, a young prostitute dying of cancer of the cervix. The tumor has eroded into her bowels and bladder so she is constantly wet and dirty. Mary has almost no visitors—certainly no friends. Her man has left her for a younger woman and her thirteen-year-old daughter is already "on the game." Poor Mary. She is her own worst enemy. She is selfish and demanding and quite blatantly manipulating all of us. It is hard to forgive the fact that just two weeks ago she was cruelly vindictive to the young husband of another of our patients who was dying. But somewhere, underneath the brittle facade of this degraded woman, there is a spark of gentleness and a delicious humor. If things had been different, if she had been loved for herself long, long ago, who knows how she might have flowered.

I do not want to go into a sociological study of how these two women's circumstances have molded them, but rather look at them with what I understand to be God's eyes. One only has to think of the God of Hosea who lures the unfaithful wife into the wilderness so that he may speak to her heart, to realize the special love God has for the sinner:

> That is why I am going to block her way with thorns,
> and wall her in so that she cannot find her way;

she will chase after her lovers and never catch up
   with them,
she will search for them and never find them.
Then she will say, "I will go back to my husband,
I was happier then than I am today.". . .
That is why I am going to lure her
and lead her out into the wilderness
and speak to her heart.

Hos. 2:8-9, 16

In the New Testament, too, there is an abundance of stories
to illustrate God's love for the weak and sinful. The most famous
are the woman taken in adultery and the Good Shepherd. One
can picture so well the woman dragged naked from her bed,
standing terrified and humiliated before the excited crowd.

> The scribes and Pharisees brought a woman along who had
> been caught committing adultery; and making her stand
> there in full view of everybody, they said to Jesus, "Master,
> this woman was caught in the very act of committing adul-
> tery, and Moses has ordered us in the Law to condemn
> women like this to death by stoning. What have you to
> say?" (John 8:3-5)

We know the story well, of course; how Jesus turned the tables
on the Pharisees by asking that whoever amongst them was without sin should cast the first stone. And then, when they had all
slunk away and he was left alone with the woman, he neither
rebuked nor condemned her but said, "Go away and don't sin
any more."

In the story of the Good Shepherd the virtuous sheep are left
singing hymns in church while the shepherd goes out into the
hills or down into the dark alleys of the inner city to search out
and bring back in triumph the one who was lost. This is the God
I meet in the gospels and the God I meet in those pastors who
seem to me to be worthy of the name. It is the God who has
come to save not the virtuous but the sinner.

How, then, do we imagine God copes with our prayers, or
lack of them, for his people? What does God do with the prayers

for Beth's healing? How on earth can we know? I am quite sure that it is right that we pray for those we love — and for those we hate — and I believe deep in my heart that no prayer is lost. On the other hand I find it impossible to believe that those who have no one to pray for them are somehow disadvantaged — that would surely be a monstrous injustice. Perhaps our prayers are shared out, like alms, at some great sorting office, being distributed to those who need them most. Or perhaps our all-powerful, all-loving, all-knowing, transcendent God has the whole world in his hands, and we pray more from our own need than from his.

A few weeks before he died from cancer the broadcaster Robert Foxcroft said something like this:

> PRAYER is asking God for the power to do his will.
> MAGIC is asking God to do your will.
> I believe in prayer rather than magic.

Another way of looking at the problem of suffering is that of the writers of the Old Testament Wisdom literature. They see suffering as sent by God to purify people, to refine them as silver in a furnace. The author of the book of Ecclesiasticus writes: "Whatever happens to you, accept it, /and in the uncertainties of your humble state, be patient, /since gold is tested in the fire, /and chosen men in the furnace of humiliation" (Ecclus. 2:4-5). A rather similar passage much beloved by Catholics and used to comfort the mourner is the beginning of the third chapter of the book of Wisdom:

> But the souls of the virtuous are in the hands of God,
> no torment shall ever touch them.
> In the eyes of the unwise, they did appear to die,
> their going looked like a disaster,
> their leaving us, like annihilation;
> but they are in peace.
> If they experienced punishment as men see it,
> their hope was rich with immortality;
> slight was their affliction, great will their blessings
> be.

God has put them to the test
and proved them worthy to be with him;
he has tested them like gold in a furnace,
and accepted them as a holocaust.

                                        Wis. 3:1-6

Has God really put them to the test? That is the question.
How can we know? Do we believe in an intervening God, in a
God who actively causes this person to have cancer or that per-
son's child to die in a road accident? I really do not know what
I believe, but the question no longer vexes me. I am quite con-
tent to remain in a state of unknowing.

What is clear, however, is that many people are purified by
suffering. I have seen it in my own life and I meet it in the
people around me. The mystery, of course, is that some people
are warped and embittered by suffering while others are
strengthened and become more loving and selfless. I believe that
an important part of the vocation of the carer is to support
people during a period of trial so that they may indeed grow
and transcend the bonds of their captivity. When I write about
spiritual growth of this sort, I sometimes take a sideways look
at myself and wonder if I am imagining it: talking pious language
to comfort myself and others. I was fascinated therefore when
a nurse with whom I work commented: "It's really such a privilege to do this work, to be with these people. The way they
grow — it's fantastic." This sort of language in fact is quite common in the hospice world. Perhaps the easiest way to explain
what I am talking about is using a case history — telling the story
of a real person's struggle with pain, fear, and impending death.

It always makes me cringe when people refer to the dying as
"they" — Do they do this, or that, in your "home"? — as though
people were stripped of their individuality by suffering a common fate or coming together as a group. Perhaps, of course, it
is just an emotional survival maneuver, a distancing, a subconscious clutching of the rabbit's foot in the hope that it will protect them from evil. But people remain individuals with their
quirks and idiosyncratic needs. They get cancer at all ages and
many of our patients are in their thirties and forties — some even
under twenty. Let me tell you about one young woman's struggle

to survive—and her triumphant letting-go and birth into new life.

Joy was around thirty-two when she developed a rare tumor in her leg. It was surgically removed and it was hoped that she was cured. Then, one day, she coughed up blood and a chest x-ray revealed that her lung was compressed by fluid. At the operation the surgeon found that the surface of her lung and the whole pleural cavity were covered with malignant deposits. This situation in fact is quite common, and if the tumor is not responsive to radiation or drugs, it is incurable. In Joy's case there was an added complication because the deposits were bleeding and nothing would stop the hemorrhage.

I first heard about her at a medical dinner when I sat with a colleague, talking "shop" as doctors do. Knowing I was interested in the emotional difficulties of the dying young he said, "We've got a terrible problem at the moment—a girl who is bleeding to death. The nurses are finding caring for her terribly difficult because she's very angry. Only this morning she said to them, 'One human being couldn't stand by and watch another bleed to death, could they?' " Exhilarated as always at the prospect of a challenge, I said boldly, "I'll help her accept death." My friend raised his eyebrow at my pride and said he'd be grateful for any help.

The next day when I went to the ward, I wondered if this time I had bitten off more than I could chew. The young woman I met in the side ward was very different from what I had imagined. Sitting bolt upright in bed, she was tense with anger and fear and in no mood to cooperate with a stranger. Knowing she would never accept my offer to come to the hospice, we gave her no choice, telling her quite truthfully that the bed was needed for another patient. That afternoon, with blood running into a special line to her heart and flowing out just as surely through her chest drain, we moved her by ambulance to the hospice. Urgently we revised the management of her equipment, for people with I-V's and chest drains are usually cared for in intensive care units, not hospices.

It would take too long to tell in detail the story of the two and a half weeks that Joy was with us before she died; gradually, when she realized that we were competent to look after her and did not intend to withdraw her life-support systems she began to trust us. I negotiated with the blood bank for more time to transfuse her, although we all knew the blood was, in practical terms, being "wasted" for it was only buying her a day of life at a time.

After gaining her confidence, there came the first break-through in the journey to acceptance. I was standing behind her one morning, examining her chest, when she asked me the question all carers find so difficult to handle: "Am I going to die?" Questions like this are so often asked when one is quite unpre-pared, perhaps thinking of something different and the temp-tation is to run away or to be falsely reassuring, telling the patient that which, at one level, they long to hear. If however one lies outright, one runs the risk of depriving the sick person of their greatest need—a companion on whom they can rely to be truthful. At that particular moment there were five of us in the room—Joy, the senior nurse on duty, two visiting nurses and myself. The nurses, well used to this work, somehow merged into the background as Joy and I engaged in dialogue. I do not recall exactly how it went, except that I spoke gently and truth-fully, responding as sensitively as I was able to her questions, overt and hidden. When I had finished, there was a bond between us that was never broken—an indefinable link between two people facing the unknown. I was completely spent. Such conversations are enormously demanding in terms of intuition and sensitivity, for one is tailoring one's conversation to the language and needs of the individual, moving as in a dance— now leading, now following, but always listening to the music.

People outside this kind of work are often caught up in what seems to be a common mythology of our culture: that if you tell people they are going to die, they will "give up hope" and die more quickly. The breaker of bad news is thus often perceived, if not as an executioner, as someone who cuts short the life that is left. In reality, of course, people vary in their reaction to such news. Sometimes it spurs them to an angry determination to fight and they set about defeating the enemy with a vigor that may buy them extra time. Some do indeed become very sad and lose their taste for fighting, but for many people it is an impor-tant watershed in which physical and emotional energies may be redeployed so that precious relationships are explored and unfinished business settled.

I was not privy to the secrets of Joy's heart, but the change in her was obvious to all. As the days passed, she changed from an angry, brittle, rather demanding young woman to someone whose calm and serenity gave life to others. From clutching desperately to life for herself, she was able to rejoice in it for others and as I went off duty for a long weekend she was able to be happy for me at the prospect of respite and fun.

We did not speak much more about her illness, for she was content to live each day as it came, and the hospice is more about living than about dying. One day, however, I went into her room as her priest came out and she smiled at me rather ruefully and said, "I've just been planning my funeral." Crossing my fingers, I replied, "It's got to be a party, Joy, it's got to be a rave up. Death's the beginning, not the end." I sat there, heart in mouth, not knowing if my words would be marvelously right or terribly wrong, but she grinned and gripped my hand and said: "You give me so much strength when you talk like that."

About a week later Joy died, very peacefully, in her sleep.

If one is going to talk about "healing" in cancer care, I think one could say that Joy was "healed." She was healed of the anger and the bitterness, the selfishness and the discontent with her very cruel situation. Not only was she healed, but she grew, spiritually and humanly, in a way which amazed us all. I have no doubt that this was the work of God. True, some of us were the channels of this healing, for surely God has no hands but ours. The work, though, was God's.

Her father, who had found her illness terribly difficult, was able to say of her death, "It was so beautiful" — and indeed it was. The growth of the spirit is perhaps the most beautiful revelation of God's love that we are privileged to see, and like all beginnings of life, it is about the secret emergence of something new and vulnerable in the darkness. In the presence of such mystery one can only bow down in awe.

⊰ 10 ⊱

OUT OF THE DEPTHS

Out of the depths have I cried unto thee, O Lord. Lord, hear my voice: let thine ears be attentive to the voice of my supplications. If thou, Lord, shouldest mark iniquities, O Lord, who shall stand? (Ps. 130:1-3)

Several years ago, with only half this book written, I became depressed and quite unable to write. I found it particularly hard since I had set aside the quiet summer months to complete the work, and there I was, midsummer, with time in hand but deserted by my muse. Eventually, in September, I forced myself to begin again and this is what I wrote:

This has been for me a grey, grey summer and my heart has drifted disconsolately like an empty tender loosed from its moorings. Unable to write for a month, because of exhaustion, I have been tossed high on the crest of the wave and pitched into troughs of despair so deep there seemed no escape, the walls black, glossy, impossible to scale. Then, just as my heart had shipped so much sadness it must certainly founder, the tide receded leaving it beached, but intact upon the shore. I sit once more at my desk overlooking Plymouth Sound. The sea is shrouded in a thick cloud of mist and the quiet morning disturbed only by the occasional wail of sirens. A few leftover holiday makers make their desultory way along the Hoe while the

rest of the world returns to work. As I watch, the mist lifts
to reveal the pleasure cruisers riding quietly at anchor. It
is the first of September and another Autumn has begun.

Is it right, I wonder, for me to write about my own experience
of darkness? Would it not be better to write dispassionately
about the problems of stress and depression in carers in general,
outlining the causes and suggesting a few remedies such as counseling, support groups, regular exercise, relaxation and a healthy
diet? Oh, that would be safer all right. Then I would be seen as
a calm knowledgeable professional, fully in control of my life
and job, and people would say, "Isn't she marvelous? So strong
and capable."

But it is my experience that people are hungry for personal
testimony; they want to know how *you* do it; how *you* keep slim,
handle your guilt about the Third World or cope with anxiety,
depression, or insomnia. As the years go by and I become in
some ways more confident about myself as a person I have
become more prepared to reveal my vulnerability and I have
come to understand that, paradoxically, in my weakness lies my
great strength. Whereas years ago I thundered eloquently from
platform and pulpit about the needs of the Third World, I now
sit and talk more gently of the yawning gulf between my ideals
and the actual realities of how I live my life. I have learned to
laugh at myself in public and share my weaknesses with others
so that they may be encouraged, rather than impressed.

More than anything I have learned that we are all frail people, vulnerable and wounded; it is just that some of us are more
clever at concealing it than others! And of course the great joke
is that it is O.K. to be frail and wounded because that is the way
the almighty transcendent God made people. The world is not
divided into the strong who care and the weak who are cared
for. We must each in turn care and be cared for, not just because
it is good for us, but because that is the way things are. The
hardest thing for those of us who are professional carers is to
admit that we are in need, peel off our sweaty socks and let
someone else wash our dirty blistered feet. And when at last we
have given in and have allowed someone to care for us, perhaps
there is a certain inertia which makes us want to cling to the

role of patient, reluctant to take up the task of serving once more. It is easy to forget that so much caring, so much serving is done by people who are weary and in some way not quite whole. Because we want our carers to be strong and invulnerable, we project on to them qualities which in fact they do not have. But again, perhaps that is the way things are because that is the way people are and we must learn to be strong for those who need us most urgently and relax and lower our guard with those who are able to accept our weakness and to cherish us.

Let me tell you a little of how it is for me. I am the youngest child of a shy artistic English gentlewoman who did not much care for children, and an ambitious, clever Australian Air Force officer who from childhood carried all before him. Now, at fifty, with both my parents long since dead, I piece together the fragments of information about them and our life together so that I may understand the woman I am today. The jigsaw is as yet incomplete, but there emerges a picture of conflicting gifts: of a powerful creativity only partially fulfilled in caring for the sick; and a terrible urge to succeed, to be better than other people, to climb every mountain, that has driven me far in my profession but leaves me still restless and hungry for more. Perhaps because I am a religious person, I understand this hunger in part as a longing for God and I am aware of the tension between the contemplative and apostolic sides of my spirit: a tension that is highly creative but easily thrown out of balance if one or another is denied its needs. These personality traits are no doubt bound up in my Irish ancestry: a Celtic temperament with its highs and lows, lyrical strands and a deep earthy pragmatism. Anyway, wherever it all comes from, I am subject to conflicting drives and wild changes in mood which vary from a feeling that I can conquer the world to a despair in which I have fantasies of ending my life. I have from time to time sought psychiatric help in the belief that I was suffering from a depressive illness but I am assured that it is no more than a deep mood swing and that much of it is under my own control. If what I experience, then, is part of the human condition and perhaps particularly common in people who, for whatever reason, drive themselves very hard, then it is worth talking about it rather than pretending it does not happen.

What seems to happen to me is that when I am high I misjudge my capacity for work and other endeavors and take on more things than I have strength for. This folly is compounded by the fact that my fertile imagination dreams up a dozen different schemes of research, broadcasting, education, or expanding and improving the care for the dying, and I then set about convincing people that I propose to implement them. Were I not also extremely articulate, this would probably not matter and I would be laughed into submission by my colleagues; but when I am in form I can convince almost anyone of the virtue and viability of my ideas!

This spring was another of those occasions when I bit off more than I could chew: lectures at home, lectures abroad, some broadcasting, a film about the hospice and the first half of this book. And it was not as if I did not complete the course: oh, I made it to the finish line all right, straining at the tape, and the crowds went wild and cheered as I lay, gasping, on the cinders. But then the crowds went home for tea and there was I, alone and shivering with a mouth full of cinders and my heart wrung out like a discarded towel.

It always takes me a long time to accept the connection between the over-spending of emotional energy and the depression that follows. If it hit me the next day, perhaps I would learn my lesson, but it does not happen that way. While I am in the middle of it all I ride high and think I am coping beautifully — but then things start to go wrong and I panic. The first thing that goes wrong is my sleep. Instead of waking around half-past six or seven, I wake at five and then four, three and two. My mind races and my guts churn and I know I am done for. The commitments of the next few months rise up in serried rows to mock me and I am mortally afraid. "Now you've done it," the voices say. "You'll make a fool of yourself and no one will ever respect you again. You'll lose your job and what'll you do then?" On and on it goes and the panic rises like gall in my throat. I force myself out of bed and go into the kitchen. The city is dark. All the world is asleep but me. No one else has insomnia like mine, grief like my grief. There is no one I can talk to. I am totally alone. No one loves me. I am a total failure. On and on it goes. I wallow in a sea of guilt, misery, and despair.

When one complains about insomnia, people often make

banal remarks like, "Just lie there and relax, it will do you as much good." Or, "Why don't you get up and write some letters, or read a book or paint a picture?" It is hard to explain that in the depths of such despair one is in no state to write letters except desperate self-pitying angry ones to a priest or counselor. I have two possible choices: I can read a medical textbook or I can pray. Mostly I pray, clutching a mug of cocoa and huddled in sweaters and blankets gazing through my tears at the flickering light of a candle. Sometimes even that is impossible and I read the Psalms of the Divine Office, trying to feel some bond with the monks and nuns who also pray at this unearthly hour. Perhaps it is no coincidence that the Psalms of Matins, now boringly called "The Office of Readings," are so often the sad, angry psalms of a people trapped by oppression or by circumstance:

> My God, my God, why have you forsaken me?
> You are far from my pleas and the cry of my distress.
> My God, I call by day and you give no reply;
> I call by night and I find no peace.
>
> Ps. 22:1-2

I am fascinated by the number of these psalms of entreaty: perhaps my experience is a much more common human phenomenon than I had realized, but people do not talk about it for fear of what others may think. However that may be, their words echo so clearly my own feelings of loneliness and despair that I can easily make them my own.

I find the same sense of bond with the poet-priest Gerard Manley Hopkins when I read "Carrion Comfort" or another of his poems of desolation, like this sonnet which begins:

> I wake and feel the fell of dark, not day,
> What hours, O what black hours we have spent
> This night! What sights you, heart, saw; ways you
>   went!
> And more must, in yet longer lights delay . . .

I find Hopkins difficult to fathom and I do not claim to plumb the depths of this poem, but rather to say that this kind of verse resonates with me when things are black. Curiously enough, it was another of his poems of desolation which helped me begin the ascent out of my most recent pit of despair. I have known "Carrion Comfort" since my school days and loved the imagery of the wrestling with God, but this time it was the first few lines that struck a chord in me, for I realized that I had given up my attempts to overcome depression and was, like Hopkins, tempted to "feast" upon my despair:

> Not, I'll not, carrion comfort, Despair, not feast on
> thee;
> Not untwist—slack they may be—these last strands
> of man
> In me or, most weary, cry *I can no more*, I can;
> Can something, hope, wish day come, not choose not
> to be.
> But ah, but O thou terrible, why wouldst thou rude
> on me
> Thy wring-world right foot rock? lay a lionlimb
> against me?
> With darksome devouring eyes my bruisèd bones?
> and fan,
> O in turns of tempest, me heaped there; me frantic
> to avoid thee and flee?
> Why that my chaff might fly; my grain lie, sheer and
> clear.
> Nay in all that toil, that coil, since (seems) I kissed
> the rod.
> Hand rather, my heart lo! lapped strength, stole joy,
> would laugh, cheer.
> Cheer whom though? the hero whose heaven han-
> dling flung me, foot trod.
> Me? or me that fought him? O which one? is it each
> one? That night, that year
> Of now done darkness I wretch lay wrestling with
> (my God!) my God.
>
> Gerard Manley Hopkins
> "Carrion Comfort"

When one is very low—or at any rate, when I am very low, I search desperately for someone to pull me out. I talk about it to those who support me and I long for some anti-depressant pill which will work a miracle and restore me to good spirits and high energy. The really hard thing to accept is that, while other people can support me and hold my hand in the darkness, it is *I* who must make the effort to struggle toward the mouth of the cave. It is I who must make the decision not to feast upon my despair, to tighten up the weary slackened sinews of resolve and determine to hope that day *will* come. It is hard, very hard, but possible. (Remember that I write of a deep mood swing, not a depressive illness.) This time I listened in a dull fury to the psychiatrist who said, "Do you take any exercise? Why don't you buy a bicycle or take up swimming! I'm sure you'd be able to sleep better if you were physically exhausted." I wanted to scream at him and say: "You don't understand—the sea is too cold, the pool's too small, I'm too exhausted. The hills are too steep to ride a bike—and anyway I hate going out alone." But this time I was too weary to argue and suddenly acquiesced. Then I went home, and, hating him and myself and all the world, dug out my bathing suit and went to swim in the open air pool.

It was cold—freezing but I suddenly noticed that the sun was bright and the water shining and the Sound was full of sailing boats skimming past like a flock of birds, their multi-colored wings gloriously filled by the light evening wind. I sat for a while and watched them and without my noticing it hope crept into my heart again. I have swum every day for three weeks now, struggling out of bed and down the steps to the sea. It is perishing cold, but oh, so beautiful and each day I feel a little stronger and my limbs move more freely. I had forgotten the view of the harbor and its ships that one gets from the raft anchored off the swimming jetty and I have learned to enjoy the fleeting, undemanding companionship of the other early morning bathers. It remains to be seen if I have the strength to brave the cold all year round: but for the moment it is enough that I am strong and well again and that I sleep.

What is the meaning, the deeper spiritual meaning, of this kind of experience? Does it have meaning at all? Perhaps, like all life, it has whatever meaning you can wrest out of it, whatever lessons you can learn. I think I can draw two major truths from my own experience of depression, exhaustion, burnout, whatever it should be called. The first is the lesson of humility. I have to learn and re-learn that I do not have the strength to do all the things I want to do. I cannot hold down a demanding full-time job, fill every spare moment with lecturing, writing and broadcasting and expect to survive. I am only human and I have very human needs. I need time to myself, I need to pray, to play, to read, to be with friends, to have fun. If I am always away or exhausted or working, how can I enter into a healthy relaxed relationship with people? And if I do not cherish my friendships, how can I expect to keep them? Again and again we religious people forget that we are only human and that we have just the same needs as the people we care for. If we are too proud or too stupid or too disorganized to take time out and care for ourselves, who will? And if we fall apart, then who will care for those who depend upon us? Do we not owe it to those we serve to accept our limitations and cherish our minds and bodies so that we will be available to serve them a little longer? I have learned to be very wary of the famous prayer of St. Ignatius:

Lord Jesus, teach me to be generous,
To give and not to count the cost,
to fight and not to heed the wounds,
To work and not to seek for rest,
Save in the knowledge that we do
your most holy will.

Is it *really* the will of God that we should deny our humanity and work ourselves into the ground? I suspect not. I am not talking about times of disaster or emergency—then surely we are all called to push ourselves to the limits of endurance. No—I am talking of routine day-to-day caring for the sick, the handicapped, or the otherwise disadvantaged. If we are to be engaged in this work for a substantial number of years then we must take time out, each day, each week, and each year. We must take days off and holidays, like the rest of men and women, because, however dedicated, we remain just that: ordinary men and women.

I say this with some passion because there is a tendency for those on the outside to think that people in the caring professions are somehow different, more dedicated and without ordinary human needs. There is a curious disparity between the voices that say "I do think the work you do is wonderful. I don't know how you do it: I certainly couldn't," and the voices (paradoxically the same!) that keep a watchdog eye on salaries, sick pay, and holidays, lest they get out of hand. The world longs for its Mother Teresa figures because it can put them safely on a pedestal and admire them, but it feels quite differently about nurses (who do the same work) belonging to a trade union and protesting about their salaries! In the past six years I and the nurses with whom I work have cared for nearly one thousand patients in a cramped ten-bed hospice. We are, I believe, by any standards, a devoted group of carers, but we have seen too often the threadbare scratchy behavior of those who are overstretched not to know that our time out is a vital part of serving. Knowing one's needs is integral to the humility of the carer.

⊰{ 11 }⊱

THE WOUNDED HEALER

*And there was one that wrestled with him until daybreak who,
seeing that he could not master him, struck him in the socket
of his hip, and Jacob's hip was dislocated as he wrestled with
him.* (Gen. 32:26)

Perhaps the most exasperating, yet at the same time the most
exciting thing about the gospels is the richness of their paradox.
Do you want to save your life, we are asked? Do you want to
live happily ever after? Well then, you must lose it first. Unless
you take up your cross you can never be happy. And, speaking
of the cross, we must not forget that the cross in Jesus' day
meant ignominious death—not just a spiritual symbol of a hard
time. Jesus' whole life in fact was a paradox: the barefoot Mes-
siah who was more at home with the outcast than the estab-
lishment, the Savior who himself became a victim of the
oppressors—and in his dying, completed his mission. Really,
when you think about it, it is very hard to take. St. Paul sums
up our difficulty when he speaks to his bemused disciples of the
folly of the gospel:

> And so, while the Jews demand miracles and the Greeks
> look for wisdom, here are we preaching a crucified Christ;
> to the Jews an obstacle that they cannot get over, to the .
> pagans madness, but to those who have been called,
> whether they are Jews or Greeks, a Christ who is the power

and the wisdom of God. For God's foolishness is wiser than human wisdom, and God's weakness is stronger than human strength. (1 Cor. 1:22-25)

The spiritual life too abounds in paradox. Just as we think we have understood something, it is turned upside down for us; the mat is pulled out from under our feet and we are left sitting on the floor muttering "but I *thought* you said . . ." Learning to live with paradox is an essential part of humility, of bowing down in baffled awe before a mysterious incomprehensible God. Thus, having written at length about the importance of accepting our limitations and taking care of ourselves in order to survive as carers, I have now to admit that every time I am forced by circumstances or my own stupidity to enter into darkness and suffering I emerge battered, but richer. As the nineteenth-century philosopher Adalbert Stifter wrote, "Pain is a Holy Angel which shows treasure to man which otherwise remains forever hidden."

What is it about pain and suffering that make them the instrument or the occasion of revelation, the gift of a loving God? We are back in the territory of the faithful God who frequently lets his friends fall sick, not because God is angry with them but precisely so that they may be purified, may learn to rest upon God alone.

There are two aspects of the experience of personal suffering which I see as relevant to Christian caring and which I wish to explore. The first is the rather pragmatic issue of empathy, of entering into a world of the client; and the second is that much more mysterious business exemplified in the Bible by Jacob's struggle with the angel: the encounter with the living God.

People often ask me if my experience of prison has helped to prepare me for my work with the dying. The answer, of course, is yes, for any major experience of powerlessness must give one some insight, however limited, into the feelings of those facing death. What do I recall of my own experience that can help me understand my patients? What does the prisoner of conscience in a Latin American jail have in common with the cancer patient? I think my strongest memory is of *fear*: the fear of pain, of helplessness, of brutality, of humiliation, of death. It was a fear that possessed me like a demon, present day and night, lurking like an animal in the shadows. It invaded my very being, rising in the throat like gall, choking like a hand around the jugular. It attacked the knees turning them to jelly so that I could barely walk and yet did. It attacked the mind, paralyzing thought, clouding my vision like the blindfold so that all landmarks disappeared and I was irrevocably disoriented and alone. It was a fear that made me want to scream out in agony, to cower like an animal, teeth bared, quivering. But of course I did not. People do not. They hang on, nerve and sinew, externally calm, wearing dignity like an armor even when their clothes have been torn away, leaving their bodies exposed and vulnerable. Outsiders sometimes speak of the degradation of prisoners – but I never felt degraded: just hurt, vulnerable and afraid. All this was hard, very hard, but I never lost hope. Even when I was afraid of dying, I believed that I would survive – and I did. So, hard as my experience was, how can I really plumb the depths of the fear of those who *know* that they are going to die? But at least I have had a taste of fear, and I can offer my hand across the void.

The second major experience as a prisoner that I share with those I care for is a feeling of *loss*. It is perhaps impossible for those who have always been in command of their lives and affairs to know what it is like to have the controls suddenly wrenched from their grasp.

> It is hard for those who have never known persecu-
> tion,
> And who have never known a Christian,
> To believe these tales of Christian persecution.
> It is hard for those who live near a Bank
> To doubt the security of their money.
> It is hard for those who live near a Police Station
> To believe in the triumph of violence.
>   T. S. Eliot
>   from *The Rock,* ch. VI

Just as it is hard for those who have always slept safely in their beds to understand what it means to lose their liberty, so it is difficult for those of us whose bodies have always answered our command, to understand what it is to have legs that neither move nor feel or a bladder over which there is no control. In prison I lost my freedom to move at will, to go to the bathroom when I needed, to eat when I was hungry, to read or write. But at least my mind remained alert and my sphincters intact. When I looked between the bars of my cell I longed for the feel of grass under my feet — for the day when I would touch it again. But the dying look out of their window at the cars and know they will never drive again. The sailors smell the sea air and know that they have held the tiller for the last time. *That* is loss. I cannot fathom it, merely skim the surface.

What I *do* share, however, is the loss of that sense of immortality, of invulnerability which is the pride of youth. Once the impossible, the unspeakable has happened, *nothing* is ever impossible again. Every creak upon the stair is an enemy, every car backfiring a machine gun, every fleeting pain a sign of cancer. But perhaps this loss is no bad thing, for it gives one a shared insecurity, a bond with the old lady who has been mugged, with the girl who was raped, with the man whose constipation turned out to be cancer. One loses the protective belief that car accidents, brain tumors and physical violence are things that happen to other people, and knows that they can happen to oneself.

As I write this it sounds rather negative and hard but I do not mean it to be so. Happiness grounded in reality is far deeper than that built upon fantasy, and suffering teaches one that happiness can catch a person unawares in the midst of deprivation and desolation. There is a certain stripping away of the externals which makes one more sensitive to joy as well as to sorrow. More of this later.

My time in prison, then, has enabled me to experience *in carne propria*, the Latins say, in my own flesh, what it is like to be unutterably alone and afraid of pain and death. In this sense I have been gifted, prepared for my work with the dying. There are, however, other much more common and rather banal experiences which have also helped me enter the world of the terminally ill. I spoke earlier of my fury at the lack of privacy in a gynecological outpatients clinic and how I felt humiliated at the exposure not of my body but of my neurotic behavior. We British have, I think, a terror of behaving badly and have somehow been indoctrinated with certain very submissive codes of behavior in relation to our medical carers. So many people, when I talk to them about dying or about the impending death of those they love, find themselves struggling with tears and almost to a person they apologize for crying and for wasting my time. It is a great joy to be able to give people permission to cry, to be angry, to be sad—to be what I like to call a paid-up member of the human race.

Psychotherapists in particular pay special attention to providing conditions in which their clients feel "safe" to be themselves. Carl Rogers, in his book *On Becoming a Person* talks about the "conditions for growth" in the therapeutic relationship. The first of these conditions is what he calls *congruence*. By this he means that the therapist, whether doctor, priest, teacher, or parent, should not only be aware of his or her own deepest feelings but should act in keeping with them. By this he means that not only should we acknowledge our feelings to ourselves but we should not hide behind a façade, pretending to be someone we are not. Our clients will only feel safe to be themselves if we are our true selves. I find that behaving in a warm and informal manner with my clients is in itself a powerful therapeutic tool, defusing much of the fear engendered by "going to the doctor." The second condition is that the therapist should exhibit *empathy*: that he or she should experience the private world of the client as if it were his or her own. The third condition for growth is what Rogers calls *unconditional positive regard*. This means in effect that our attitude to our client is without judgment. We leave them space to be angry, to talk of their dark side, safe in the knowledge that nothing they say or do will make us reject them. They are freed from the terror that if they reveal too much of themselves or say "the wrong thing" the doctor/priest will freeze and become pompous or angry and show them the door.

The fourth and last condition is that we allow the client to *experience* something of our congruence, our empathy, and our unconditional positive regard. It is no good caring deeply for people and concealing this behind a barrier of icy professional detachment. If people do not *know* themselves cared for, they will be prey to a thousand fears of being misunderstood or rejected. Having experienced this kind of care myself from priests and other professional carers, I know that the feeling of security and affirmation engendered is enormously healing. I believe it is one of the most important ways we can experience and mediate Christ's love.

I believe too that it is easier to be open and sensitive to people in this way if we have experienced some of the small fears and humiliations to which they are subject.

A recent severe asthmatic attack gave me a small taste of the terror of those who fight for enough breath to stay alive, and also of the awful anxiety and indecision of the half-way stage in which one does not know if one is bad enough to call the doctor and if he will think one is a fool for calling him in the middle of the night. Hard too was the experience of the brisk young doctor who stood at the foot of my bed in the hospital and said, "I'm sure you'd like to go home"—when I could not face either the prospect of being alone or being a "burden" on my family and friends.

Enough. Hard as it is to be ill, I find that each episode, when it is over, has been in some sense a gift. It has taught me a little more about myself and about people in general and it has given me another tool with which to practice my art. I like to think that the wounded healer is more sensitive and compassionate than those who are strong and "whole."

There is, however, another quite different aspect to the personal experience of suffering which has relevance to the way we function as carers, and that is the way in which suffering can be for us an encounter with the living God. This is a very mysterious business which is not easy to write about for the experience is by no means constant and universal. Clearly, severe personal suffering is for some people a disaster, destroying their faith both in God and in human nature, leaving them permanently damaged and embittered. Others, however, are immeasurably strengthened and transformed as people, becoming filled with a peace and generosity which makes them almost incandescent and a source of strength to those they meet. One such person was Margaret, a woman in her fifties who spent three months with us at the hospice before she died. The cancer which afflicted her spread to her bones, weakening them so that they fractured and in her last weeks she had fractures of her spine, leg, and arms. Unable to turn over in bed or move her hands more than a few inches, she spent her days for others. She arranged presents for all those she loved: a painting of their favorite picnic spot for her husband; an enlarged photograph for me and so on. For a long time she set her heart on going home, but when she realized that this was impossible, she accepted it and turned her gaze outwards, rejoicing in the comings and goings of her family and staff. Immobile, incontinent, in pain, she was a woman supremely in control of herself, giving strength to all who came to her bedside. It would come as no surprise to hear that Margaret was a woman of deep Christian faith who had put her trust in God and was sustained by him. As it happened, however, she had no faith in God or in a life hereafter. Throughout her illness she remained firm in her belief that her death would be the end. Her faith was in love and in people and that was enough to sustain her in what seemed to be a heroically selfless life.

I tell this story because it is so important that we Christians do not delude ourselves that we have a monopoly on goodness. I have met many generous Christian nurses and doctors but many more equally selfless non-believers. The spirit of God knows no cultural, national, or denominational boundaries.

Once again it seems appropriate to write from personal experience of suffering and what it has taught me. This time I write of the intangible, the unknowable: of what I understand as an encounter with God. The experience is one which has changed my life in that it has given me a sort of carnal knowledge, a gut level conviction of an all-powerful, loving God. This conviction is, I believe, the greatest gift that I bring to my work, enabling me somehow to sustain those who are afraid and in pain.

My particular encounter with God happened in the context of solitary confinement in prison—but it could just as well have been after a major accident, an illness or bereavement. The essence of the situation was that it was an experience of stripping and of powerlessness, which made me more aware, more open to the presence of God.

It happened like this. After I had been arrested and interrogated by the secret police for treating a wounded revolutionary, I was moved from the torture center to another prison and placed in solitary confinement. Here, left to my own devices and with the constant harassment of the interrogation behind me, I found that, for the first time since my arrest, I had sufficient emotional and intellectual space to maneuver, to choose what to do. My immediate inclination was to scream out to God for help, to batter spiritually on the bars of my cage, begging to be released. Surely I who was planning to devote my life to him as a nun must be specially loved and able to ask his favor? Then a very curious thing suggested itself to me: while I knew that it was quite right and proper that I should besiege heaven with my prayers to be released, an even better way would be to hold out my empty hands to God, not in supplication but in offering. I would say, not "Please let me out" but, "Here I am Lord, take me. I trust you. Do with me what you will." In my powerlessness and captivity there remained to me one freedom: I could abandon myself into the hands of God. Perhaps it was no coincidence that I received from a friend a book containing the following poem:

Abandonment

What is an abandonment experience?
Is it leaving oneself on God's doorstep,
    walking into the rest of life,
        not allowing anxiety,
            fear,
                frustration to enter into one?
Is it expecting God to keep one warm,
            secure,
            and safe,
            unharmed?
Is that abandonment?

Abandonment has nothing to do with warmth
            of womb or arms
            or close clasped hearts.

It is not something done by a child.
It is done to him.

It cannot be done to an adult.
It is done by him.
Abandonment is committed only with and in the
   maturity of Christ Jesus.
It is not just a hanging loose.
It is a letting go.
It is a severing of the strings by which one
   manipulates,
         controls,
         administrates
      the forces in one's life.
Abandonment is receiving all things the way
   one receives
      a gift
   with opened hands,
   an opened heart.

Abandonment to God
   is the climactic point in any man's life.

Anon., in Edward Farrell
Disciples and Other Strangers

So for the next three weeks I struggled to let go the strings of my life, to hand myself over to God. It was not a once and forever dramatic gesture, but a long and terrible struggle, a wrestling with an unseen stranger in the dark hours of the night. The fight had begun some months before in the grounds of a retreat house outside Santiago when I had taken a week apart to pray and discern whether or not I had a vocation to become a nun. It was then that I had conceived the idea of my life as a bank check to be made payable to God, the amount and the time of cashing being left to the drawer. It had seemed hard then, as I lay in tears on a pile of autumn leaves and made my "fiat," but it was in some sense a pious game. Now, however, my bluff was being called. I had made my life over to God then, so did I now wish to withdraw that offer? Were there strings attached to my gift, conditions to my loving? Day after day I struggled. Sometimes I snatched the check back and tore it in half or threw it to the floor; then at other times, when my tears were spent, I would pick it up and, smoothing the stained paper, tape the torn fragments together and hand it over again. How many times this drama enacted itself I do not know, but there came a day when I no longer wanted to take the check back and I was able to make my own the prayer of St. Ignatius, "Grant that I may love thee always, then do with me what thou wilt."

This abandonment experience of mine of course took place in the rather melodramatic context of a Chilean jail, but it could equally well have happened in a British hospital, a convent, or a suburban house. The act was an interior one, a spiritual maneuver taking place within the confines of physical power-lessness. This option for abandonment is available to all who find themselves trapped by circumstance and is the means by which the imprisoned can transcend their bonds. Like a bird in a cage they can choose to exhaust themselves battering their wings against the bars — or they can learn to live within the con-fines of their prison and find, to their surprise, that they have the strength to sing. Those who are given the courage to accept their situation find that they have far greater reserves of emo-tional energy than they had realized, for that strength which they had hitherto exhausted in a vain effort to escape is now available to them to adapt to their situation. Helping people accept what is happening to them is an important part of my work with the dying and it involves, not, as is commonly thought, a giving up of struggle, but a letting go in order to grow and be free.

At the beginning of this passage on abandonment I spoke boldly of an encounter with God. It is difficult to speak clearly of this kind of experience. It is not a question of visions or voices, but, like Jacob, one knows that one has wrestled all night with a stranger, and as daylight breaks, emerged limping but some-how blessed.

⊰ 12 ⊱

LIVING IN UNITY

How good and how pleasant it is,
When brothers live in unity!

Ps. 133:1

Having written at some length of the experience of personal suffering and the manner in which it both humbles and shapes us, I turn to another very important cause of pain in carers: interpersonal conflict. As in the rest of this book, I do not offer clear answers—just a few recollections from someone in the middle of a particular situation: a small hospice for the terminally ill.

The first thing that must be said is that conflict is endemic in communities, and that not only is it a cause of much individual suffering, but it can be very damaging to the work of the group. The next observation is that this conflict is frequently hidden from the casual observer—patients or families cared for in a hospice, retreatants in a guest house or visitors to a monastic community. I have often shared with friends involved in retreat work or other communities the wry humor they feel when visitors exclaim, "What a marvelous atmosphere—you can feel it as soon as you come in!" One smiles enigmatically and makes no comment, hoping devoutly that the tense voices behind the closed door will remain inaudible and that the scars on one's heart can be concealed just a little longer.

Gerard Manley Hopkins in his poem *In the Valley of the Elwy* captures that very special feeling of welcome that some houses can evoke in the visitor:

> I remember a house where all were good
> To me, God knows deserving no such thing:
> Comforting smell breathed at very entering,
> Fetched fresh, as I suppose off some sweet wood.
> That cordial air made those kind people a hood
> All over, as a bevy of eggs the mothering wing
> Will, or mild nights the new morsels of spring:
> Why, it seemed of course, seemed of right it should.

I have long thought that this poem referred to St. Beunos, the massive Jesuit house in the Clwyd valley where Hopkins wrote much of his poetry, and where from time to time I have found refuge when my heart was troubled. He is, however, referring *not* to this religious community but to some friends in London! On reflection this comes as no surprise because Hopkins was too close to his own community not to be painfully aware of the disharmony behind the welcoming façade.

I write *façade* for that is what it is: we present quite unconsciously to the stranger a warmth and welcome which is only one facet of the truth of our community life. We allow them to share, for a time, in our riches of love and companionship, but shield them from the painful forces by which we are being shaped as a group of people. Like the whole of creation, we are groaning in a great travail. God is at work in us, stripping, hollowing, molding, purifying, in a process which is infinitely painful but without which we would never become a community. I find it rather a joke that I, who after twenty years "vocationitis" found that I was quite unsuited to religious life, should end up, after all, in the heart of a community of women. If one believes in a God who "writes straight with crooked lines," then perhaps the eighteen months I spent as a novice was a formation, not as I had intended, for starting my own monastic community, but for being the medical director of a cancer hospice! Let me share with you my experience of community life, for what it lacks in depth it makes up for in variety!

My first experience of community, like so many Catholic

schoolgirls, was a boarding school run by nuns. In the early 1950s Catholics rejoiced in an intellectual security concerning the ways of God which the Second Vatican Council was to explode for ever. The nuns *knew* with a deep certainty that the religious life was the highest possible way of serving God and that anyone who had a "vocation – a calling" to become a nun was especially loved by God.

It should come as no surprise therefore that many of the more ambitious or susceptible of us became stricken with what has become known as the "divine measles": the belief that God was calling us to the religious life. My own attack came in the middle of a quite blatant "vocations" retreat in which we were plunged into prayer in order to reflect upon our immortal souls. Surrounded by posters with legends such as "We grow like those with whom we live – the nun lives with Christ," or the recruiting-poster demand, "Is God calling YOU to the religious life?," perhaps it is no wonder that it has taken me nearly forty years to be convinced that I am running, *not* away from God but *towards* him. I know now that my vocation, my best way of serving God, lies not in a convent but in lovingly doing that task for which I am best equipped.

But of course it was not only the vocations drive which convinced me I should become a nun: it was the fact that I recognized in those particular women qualities of warmth and generosity that I had not met in those outside the convent. Whatever the quality of their community life, they gave me a glimpse of something so special that I was to spend the next twenty-five years in its pursuit.

My next experience of community was, I suppose, in the 1960s when I was first a medical student and then a resident in the Radcliffe Infirmary in Oxford. Perhaps it is stretching it a bit to call a big hospital a community – and yet we were bonded together as a group of people in the service of our patients. I was a resident in the "bad" old days when junior doctors had no time off and we worked and slept and ate and found our fun within the confines of the hospital. I remember that, arriving late for work on the first morning, I left my bicycle outside the main door of the hospital – only to find it gone when I emerged to claim it three months later! But, in spite of it all, my memories of that first year as a doctor are tinged with an immense nostalgia. There was a sense of pride of belonging to a great and worthwhile enterprise that made one put up with appalling hours of work, bad food and poor living conditions; there was, too, an amazing sense of comradeship that bound us together in a way which does not seem to happen today when many young doctors are married or only on call every third or fourth night. I am not saying it was better in my day, just different. There was also a curious loyalty between people far distant from each other in the hierarchical structure. I suppose it was a very paternalistic world but I remember with real affection the domestic staff who cherished us in a way that is less common in today's more egalitarian society. I would not deny that the great hospitals of twenty years ago were full of proud doctors and underpaid porters but we shared an *esprit de corps* that is less obvious today. And what of conflict in those day? I have no memory of deep feuds—just the odd row between people who were tired and cross. In hindsight I would suspect that there *was* conflict and hurt among the senior doctors, because it seems there always is—but this would not necessarily have been apparent to us as junior doctors. There was too the time-honored hierarchical structure by which people protected their own emotional space while in the hospital and which led to a slightly formal, stylized way of relating to each other which was not unlike behavior patterns in the armed forces or in a monastery.

I must admit that having long mocked the hierarchical barriers in medical and clerical society I am, in my middle years, coming to appreciate their value! It is not easy to be in a position of authority, still less to be a good leader; and perhaps a certain distance and formal way of relating makes it easier to remain impartial in disputes and to correct when that is necessary. There is too the very basic fact that each of us has only a limited amount of emotional energy and one cannot be all things to all men. I am certainly not advocating the sort of society in which those in authority are allowed to be pompous and arrogant but rather some sort of compromise between two ways of being. Alas, nothing is ever black or white, much as we would like it so!

I spent a number of years in these curious medical "communities," working all the hours God gave, and playing just as hard in between times. One of my happiest years was spent at the Churchill Hospital in Oxford where I was a resident in surgery. We lived in old Nissen huts left over from the war years when the Churchill had been an American army hospital. They were incredibly ugly but well heated and we were not very demanding in those days. If we were not demanding, however, we made up for it by satisfying our needs by devious means and the authorities turned a blind eye so long as the work got done and we did not burn the place down. There was one particular time when the dozen or so of us in my hut were united in our law breaking. With my philosophy that nothing is impossible until proven so, I was probably one of the ringleaders.

It happened like this. After finishing a particularly exhausting six-month stint in the accident and emergency department at the Radcliffe, I was given a week's leave before beginning my next job as senior house officer in plastic surgery at the Churchill Hospital. When I arrived, refreshed from my week in Devon, I found that Consuelo, a Chilean doctor in the U.K. on a British Council scholarship, had done my locum. We became good friends and I discovered that she was living a cold and lonely existence in a bed-sit in Headington. This seemed nonsense when she belonged with us junior doctors and when we discovered there was a spare bed stored in the box-room we assembled it and moved her in among the suitcases. We got away with it for nearly a month but then the cleaning lady complained to her supervisor. (Did I write rather sentimentally a few pages ago about doctors being cherished by adoring domestic staff? Perhaps the Churchill was different!) We were not to be easily thwarted, however, and I hit on a brilliant idea. The resident in thoracic surgery was a married woman called Phil who had for many years been a psychotherapist and was getting a medical qualification so that she could practice as a psychiatrist. We decided that it was bad for Phil's marriage that she be apart from her husband, so every night we packed her off home in Consuelo's elderly Ford, "Harry" (named after Henry Ford, of course), while Consuelo slept in her bed and took her night calls. When I moved on to general surgery, Consuelo got the plastic surgery job and for a while we were all legal, but then my job finished and it was I who had nowhere to sleep. Nothing daunted, we picked a clean bed, mattress and armchair off the hospital skip and set up house in Consuelo's room. As we wearied of hospital food we took up housekeeping seriously and one Saturday afternoon moved a fridge and small cooker in through the window. Those were the days of the squatters! While I camped in Consuelo's room Australian Danny, the obstetrics and gynecology resident, had his wife and baby living with him while another houseman had a beautiful Chinese girlfriend to cook his dinner and warm his bed. Lord, we had fun!

So the conflicts in those days were with Authority, deviousness leading to almost open warfare, as on the occasion when I spent a happy Sunday morning sawing the end off my bed to convert it into a divan and found myself before the administrator on Monday morning! Feminine wiles, however, are not easily defeated and I fled with my case to a more senior official and ended up drinking sherry with him in the boardroom. This mentality was to stand me in good stead nearly ten years later when I found myself once more confined to barracks—this time in a Chilean concentration camp.

When I first arrived at Tres Alamos detention camp, after four days in an interrogation center and three weeks in solitary confinement, there were a hundred and twenty women packed into a single compound. We slept seven to a room which measured about nine feet square—perhaps less. Six of us had bunks; the seventh, Cristina (now a doctor in the U.K.), slept on the floor. The five weeks I spent with these mainly Marxist prisoners of conscience was, I think, my most impressive experience of community, outstripping by far my later experience of life in a convent. It is hardly surprising, I suppose, for prisoners of conscience are a very specially selected group of people who are not only strongly idealistic but courageous and highly disciplined. What really impressed me then, and the memory remains bright to this day, was the experience of a truly loving and sharing community. I remember Anita Maria who, when my hair fell into my dinner for the third time, handed me a hair grip—the only one she had, from her own hair. *This* was true sharing—giving away what you are using, not what is surplus to requirements. It is hard not to be nostalgic about those days. There was a kind of purity about them as, stripped of all that we had, we were welded into one body, giving graciously to the weaker members that which we would have preferred to keep for ourselves. I truly believe that, for a time, we were living a kind of basic Christian community life. How long it could have lasted one cannot say. It was enough to have experienced it, and for that I am grateful.

It was, I suppose, naive to expect that I would recapture the spirit of Tres Alamos prison in a British convent—but I did expect it when, afire with zeal about the ideal of the monastic life and full of preconceived ideas of how it should be lived, I moved from Ampleforth Abbey to become a novice in a semi-enclosed monastic convent. I found the experience very traumatic and was asked to leave after eighteen months because it was clear that I was unsuited to the life.

It is very difficult indeed to write dispassionately and honestly about the religious life. Some people write from the outside, often rather sentimentally, and I think do nuns little service. Others write after they have leapt over the wall and describe their experience with ill-concealed bitterness. Such books are often sensationalized by the Sunday papers and written off by the devout as the rantings of an unhinged and malicious mind. Even now after seven years I am loath to write about my own experience in the convent for to do so would be to risk wounding a group of women who took me to their hearts and shared everything they had with me. The fact remains, however, that I was often (though not always) terribly unhappy. I felt like a caged bird and fretted for the open spaces, for my friends and for intellectual stimulus. I badly missed the swift exchange of repartee and intellectual argument that I had known at Ampleforth and buried myself in books of history and theology. I found myself endlessly restricted by a world in which almost anything I did by instinct seemed to be wrong and I was either interiorly cowering and trying to be something I was not or relaxing and getting into trouble yet again.

I still do not really understand what was wrong. I know now quite clearly that I was not personally suited to that particular community, though I shared their *ideals* totally. It is not so much the ideals but the living out that is in question. The thing in particular that happens in convents is that there is a leaning over backwards not to upset the older members of the community. This means that out-dated and even foolish ideas and ways of living can be perpetuated out of a mistaken concept of charity. Then, of course, by the time the old guard have gone, the coming generation have become so used to the status quo that there is no longer any desire or energy for change.

Paradoxically, the other thing which is evident in some enclosed convents is a lack of ordinary Christian charity. In theory a religious community should be a place where gospel values are lived out in a very special way; it should be a witness to the power and beauty of the Christian message. More than anything a convent or monastery should be a community of love, a living out of Christ's words at the Last Supper.

> My little children . . .
> I give you a new commandment:
> love one another;
> just as I have loved you,
> you must also love one another.
> By this love you have for one another,
> everyone will know that you are my disciples.
>   John 13:33-35

But alas this is not always so. As someone who has been particularly interested in religious life I have, over the years, come into contact with quite a number of women who were either going into or coming out of enclosed convents, and I am shocked and saddened at what I hear. There emerges a picture of small-minded behavior and an obsessive preoccupation with petty material detail which would be laughable if it were not so damaging. Women who should be friends, sharing their ideals, supporting each other and growing in compassion and wisdom become somehow turned in on themselves, dried up and warped until it seems they are incapable of love. Particularly frightening is that power of the superiors in some of these very enclosed houses. Charismatic, strong women who should be educating, enabling, and liberating their charges seem to become transformed into dictators, inspiring a degrading subjection and even fear. The power of "Our Mother" over adult women, many of whom have held powerful and important posts "in the world," would be laughable — if it were not downright dangerous. The human psyche is a marvelous and fragile thing and to subject it to deforming forces in the name of Christ must surely be blasphemy.

I write thus not of my own experience but of what I have been told by strong intelligent women whose confidences I have been privileged to receive. The nuns with whom I lived for eighteen months were very good to me, struggling to help without crushing. The superiors were sane, wise women, deeply spiritual and full of humor who listened to me patiently and tried to give me space to be myself: and yet it is a fact that I *felt* far more hurt and angry when I left the convent than when I came out of prison and it took me many months before I was able to work again.

What is it then that happens to women whose extraordinary generosity and zeal for Christ has led them to give up so much of what the human race holds dear? Are they deluded, victims of childhood repression, or have they been brainwashed by religious propaganda? Or are they perhaps just ordinary people with an extraordinary longing for God who, in giving their lives to Christ, unwittingly subject themselves to a system which is inherently flawed? I believe that the latter is the case: not that the rules of St. Benedict, of St. Augustine or of Carmel are flawed but that the way in which they are interpreted leads sometimes to an unhealthy way of life. To illustrate what I mean, here is an account of convent life taken from *The Christian Neurosis* by Pierre Solignac, a French psychiatrist with twenty years experience in working with priests and nuns. The quotation comes from the testimony of a religious sister who, at the age of sixty, consulted Solignac for depression:

> I was just twenty when I became a novice. I followed a divine call which I never doubted, and I was resolved to go through with it to the end. Some basic themes kept recurring in the instructions given by the novice mistress: "You are never wrong to obey. You must be faithful in the little things. You must always ask permission." And it was

necessary to ask permission for everything: to take a bath twice a month, to wash one's hair, change one's nightdress once a month. It was also necessary to ask permission to give or receive the least little thing, even a picture; to write a letter (of course all the correspondence was censored); to go to bed or to get up at a different time than anyone else: recreation, the refectory, the religious office. Permission was also needed to have a conversation with a pupil or sister. Breaking the rule meant certain traditional penances: kissing the feet of one's sisters; eating meals on one's knees; prostrating oneself full length for all the sisters to walk over; saying a prayer in the refectory with arms outstretched; holding a pencil between one's teeth for a certain time as a punishment for breaking silence; carrying round one's neck the pieces of an article one had been clumsy enough to break. It was the done thing to ask permission to inflict certain mortifications on oneself: self-flagellation with knotted rope, or wearing bracelets made of thorns.

When I think back to this period I am struck by the fact that we were treated as though we were irresponsible, creatures who could not be trusted; the novice-mistress and the Mother Superior could enter our cells without knocking at any time. We had to leave the doors of our cells open to undress; the novice-mistress came to shut them personally, at nine in the evening. We were not allowed to go out of the garden and we were forbidden to look out of the windows giving on to the street. In the parlor there was always a sister as chaperon. We were not allowed to talk to a priest or a religious outside the confessional. Of course, all that is going back forty-five years, but it is not long since the changes came. This period of the novitiate wasn't the hardest. I followed the path laid down for me with the fixed idea, "The will of the Mother Superior is the will of God." As I wanted beyond all doubt to be faithful to God, or rather to Jesus, I did not raise any questions, and I lived day by day in a kind of unconsciousness bordering on a degree of fatalism.

This nun was sixty when she was presented to Dr. Solignac for the treatment of depression, so perhaps one could calculate that she entered the convent in the 1930s (the book was published in 1976). She is then speaking of life that existed some fifty years ago and which could be regarded as a regrettable historical fact. Indeed, Sister Prue Wilson, in her delightful book *Father Took Me to the Circus*, writes of her experience as a novice in the 1940s as a way of life which no longer exists:

> There was, too, the satisfaction of knowing that only the love of God would induce one to wear a night cap or leap out of bed well before dawn on a winter's morning. My sorrow is that although much of the life was neither good nor bad, merely peculiar, too much energy was wasted on conforming to the minutiae, and too much creativity on the need to walk a traditional tightrope acceptable to the elders of the congregation. I am not only thinking of the novices but of those asked to direct them. For us at the receiving end, most of it was either dotty or funny—the doing of it—the failure to do it, the scoldings and "penances"—all made for a bond of laughter and friendship, and tears, and a shared way of faith. But was it really worth the fuss? There were also those who were unable to laugh, who took the whole thing with a terrible seriousness. For them it proved damaging. Lives could be scarred and maturity impeded by over-concentration, not on the music or rhythm of the dance, but on its toe-pointing demands.

Karen Armstrong, in *Through the Narrow Gate*, gives a graphic account of life in a pre-Vatican II convent and of the damage that it wrought in her:

> All afternoon I had felt sick, gripped by a fierce, unreasoning terror. Now, in the hot silence of an August evening, I stood shivering slightly in the community refectory. I could feel a tumult inside me threatening to erupt. The only sounds in the vast room were the clash of heavy metal dishes and tinkling of cutlery as three white-aproned nuns scurried round, putting supper out on the long wooden

tables, their rubber soles squeaking on the polished floor. A long sunbeam slashed through the tall windows, catching the big crucifix in a dramatic natural flood light, tinging the white walls with a pink glow. Suddenly I heard a strange keening noise, a scream like an animal caught in a trap. What was it? Where was it coming from? Then, from a long way off I saw myself, my eyes clenched tightly shut, my mouth gaping and contorted and from it coming the unearthly cry. Nuns hurried round. They slapped me, shook me, but could not quell the sound. Finally I watched myself crumble through their arms in an awkward huddle. The sound stopped, and a black shutter clicked down in my brain.

The rigid inhuman system which broke Karen Armstrong in the 1960s is now ancient history in her order—but it is still alive and well today in some enclosed houses. I have spent many hours listening to accounts of convent life which bear an uncanny resemblance to that described by Armstrong or Solignac. True, many of the "dotty" customs have been abandoned, but there remains a way of handling people which is based on a false theological premise: that the will and spirit of the disciple must be broken in order that the person may be remolded. "Only when her old worldly self has been smashed to pieces can God build from the rubble a new, Christ-centered individual" (Karen Armstrong, *Through the Narrow Gate*). I see this kind of thinking as a total corruption of the Christian message, a denial of the infinite worth of the individual and the command that we should love one another. I believe it is a matter of grave scandal in the Catholic church.

It must be clearly stated, however, that there are many convents where happy mature women live together a life of community which they have freely chosen. The monastic way of life is older than Christianity itself and there will always be men and women whose desire for the transcendent God leads them to abandon home and loved ones for a life dedicated entirely to the search for God. These are what a monk friend of mine called "the God struck," those with a "vocation," a calling that they cannot deny. What seems important to me is that we Christians of the twentieth century should use our knowledge of theology and psychology to revitalize and heal a time-honored way of life that in some places has, despite the good will of many, become flawed.

There are indeed many religious communities who have done just this, and in obedience to the spirit of *aggiornimento* of the Second Vatican Council they have returned to the vision of their founders.

These women have, often painfully, examined their way of life, and are grappling with what it means to live a life consecrated to God in the latter part of the twentieth century. During the last year that I spent in Chile I became friendly with a number of American missionary sisters and found in them a marvelous amalgam of common sense and desire for God. Two of my dearest friends were Maryknoll Sisters, Ita Ford and Carla Piette. Ita, an ex-journalist, was a small woman with short dark hair and a sharp wit, while Carla was a tall, zany, artistic redhead who had caused chaos in her early days in Chile by confusing the Spanish words for charity and chastity, when she was making her confession. I remember her laughter as she described the horror of the elderly Chilean priest when a young, fully-habited American sister confessed to having sinned *contra la castidad*. It took her half an hour to extricate herself in broken Spanish while the rest of the sisters waited their turn in the line!

By the time I met them Ita and Carla had long since abandoned their religious habits and convent fortress and lived with another sister in a little wooden house in a shantytown called La Bandera on the outskirts of Santiago. I was captivated by their warmth and humor and began to wonder if here at last were women with whom I could live as sisters. We met many times in the months between Easter and my arrest in November, sharing food, good conversation and prayer in their "convent" or, more often, in my more spacious house in the suburbs. I remember particularly the times we spent sitting on the floor of my bedroom with a candle and praying that I might be freed of my attachment to my material possessions. The three of us were to laugh together again, but in another place, when that prayer was "answered" in a way that none of us had bargained for: by my being arrested and the secret police stealing anything that was of any value!

The sense of community that I experienced with these women during my last weeks in Chile was and is very precious to me. Each visiting day at Tres Alamos there would be a group of nuns and priests bearing fruit, books, sweaters, and anything else I might need. We sat on the ground and talked endlessly or walked slowly around the prison courtyard if we had need to speak of more personal things. My last memories of Ita and Carla are of those slow measured walks and the incredible urgency with which we shared the deepest meaning of my torture and imprisonment.

I just missed seeing Carla again in 1976 when I was in the United States and she was on retreat. I asked to meet her but she felt that it would be wrong to interrupt her retreat. Instead she sent me a little handkerchief embroidered with the copihue, the Chilean national flower, and a cryptic note saying something like "It's a marvelous thing to be on a journey, not knowing where you are going, especially if you trust the cabbie."

Carla's journey was to end much sooner than she or any of us expected, for in August 1980 she was drowned in El Salvador when the jeep she and Ita were traveling in was overturned in a flash flood. They had been taking a freed prisoner home because other refugees did not trust him and were afraid that he would betray them. It was this generous act that cost Carla her life and Ita her closest friend, for as they were crossing the river the torrent swelled and the jeep was overturned. Carla pushed Ita out of the window, but must have been trapped herself, for finally, "close to noon the Red Cross found her. Her broken, twisted, naked body had been washed up on a sand bar in the now tame river, fourteen kilometers from where the jeep had foundered the night before" (from *The Same Fate as the Poor* by Judith Noone, MM).

So Carla, who had driven off into the unknown, placing her trust in "the cabbie," had come home. By one of those strange quirks of fate that send shivers down the spine, I have a poem of hers, a meditation on the 23rd Psalm:

> Near restful waters He leads me — to revive
> my drooping spirit

Waters of Mountains — Waters of God
cleanse us, renew us so shabbily shod.
Rios de Chile, streams of burnt snow
melt us, tow us beyond friend or foe.
Currents so fast, pools deep and clear
tune us, quiet our hearts still to hear.
Lord of the river, God of the stream
teach us your song, our dryness redeem.

It is only now, as I transcribe this poem from the original,
that I notice that after the quote from Psalm 22 (Grail) she has
put "Ps. 123." I presume it is a slip of the pen — but on glancing
at Psalm 123 in the Gelineau translation I am struck by the
second verse:

Then would the waters have engulfed us,
the torrent gone over us.
Over our head would have swept
the raging waters.

Carla was buried in Chalatenango, among the people she had
served, and Ita had time to grieve for her friend:

Carla and I had talked lots of times about the possibility
of our dying because of things here, very violent things.
We talked about how difficult it would be if we weren't
together for the one left behind. At the very end of St.
John's Gospel there is a little scene of Jesus with Peter,
and John seems to be in the background. Jesus says to
Peter, "Follow me." Peter turns around and says, "What
about him?" And Jesus says, "I'm telling you to follow me
and he's to wait 'til I return." If John was in hearing distance, how did he feel? I think we know now. (*The Same
Fate as the Poor*)

I quote this passage from one of Ita's letters not only because
I find it moving, but because it illustrates the open nature of the
loving relationship between the two sisters. To set this in context
we must remember that there are still convents in which "par-

ticular friendships"—close friendships—between nuns are forbidden on the grounds that the nun's heart must be exclusively for Christ. It is this blinkering of the heart which is so damaging to the very people whose love of God should be opening them up to deeply human loving relationships.

Ita continued to work in Chalatenango among the refugees with Maryknoll Sister Maura Clarke who had volunteered to replace Carla. It was demanding, exhausting work involving daily contact with violence and death. They made constant trips into the countryside to deliver supplies or to pick up refugees. More often than not, Ita and Maura went along on these trips because the visibility of these paleskinned "gringo" women, particularly if they happened to be citizens of the United States, was considered a guarantee of safety to the driver and to the refugees.

One day they were called to the parish house in the environs of a town called Adeleita where sixty people had taken refuge. After unloading the sacks of grain the women and the old men told their story. For eight months they had had to sleep in the hills in the rain and cold in fear of night visits from government-sponsored death squads or the early morning army invasions. They would dare to go down to their homes only in the daylight and with a neighbor on guard so as not to be caught by security forces. Just the day before, a patrol raided their village leaving word that the next time they were going to finish off the women and children. That night all the people abandoned the area for good and trekked five hours through the night guided by the sons and husbands who were defending the area, until they finally reached the parish house at dawn. One woman gave birth to twins an hour after their arrival.

Each day the horror of the repression came closer to the sisters, its reality branded upon their hearts. One day Ita was alone in the house when a young woman came to ask her to accompany her to view the body of her son who had been killed by the security forces. Jean Donovan and Ita went with the mother to a little plot of land outside town where a farmer was digging to uncover the body.

Several minutes later he reached down into the grave to remove a handkerchief he had placed on the boy's face when he buried him two days before. "That is my son," the mother cried, "now I can rest for I know he is at peace with God." Ita trembled and tried to remove that sight from her memory. (*The Same Fate as the Poor*)

I spoke in an earlier chapter of the paradox of the spiritual life and these descriptions of the life of the missionaries in El Salvador illustrate a hard fact: that Christianity is purified and strengthened by hardship and persecution. Had Ita Ford entered an enclosed convent in Brooklyn perhaps she, like so many other women, would have become caught up in the minutiae of community life and worship and ensnared by the traps of a life lived in isolation from the world. Perhaps she had an insight into this when she wrote to a friend, "We keep plugging along here, because life is threatened by other evils worse than death—hatred, manipulation, violence and selfishness."

In November 1980 Ita and Maura flew to Nicaragua for a meeting of their congregation. At first Ita was very depressed and appeared to have no heart for discussion or celebration. Then, as the week wore on she seemed to reach some kind of turning point in her grieving process and was better able to join in the meeting. On the last night, at the closing liturgy, Ita was asked to read a passage that was important to her. She chose an excerpt from one of Archbishop Romero's homilies:

Christ invites us not to fear persecution because, believe me, brothers and sisters, one who is committed to the poor must risk the same fate as the poor. And in El Salvador we know what the fate of the poor signifies: to disappear, to be tortured, to be captive and to be found dead. (Oscar Romero, Homily for February 17, 1980)

Oscar Romero, the conservative priest radicalized by his episcopal ministry to a suffering people clearly had no illusions about the risks he was running in openly denouncing oppression. This sermon was to prove prophetic when just over a month later, on March 24, 1980, the Archbishop was assassinated while saying Mass.

Now, ten months after his death, an American woman from

Brooklyn was choosing to make his prophetic words her own. The next day, December 2, Ita and Maura flew to San Salvador. Already their names were on a death list shown covertly to the sacristan in Chalatenango. By midnight it was all over, for the two nuns disappeared after leaving the airport. At around ten that night, along the old dusty road to San Pedro Nonualco, one hour from the airport and in the opposite direction toward La Libertad, three peasants watched from a pineapple field as a white van drove by. It traveled another seven hundred yards and then stopped. The peasants heard machine-gun fire followed by single shots. Fifteen minutes later the same vehicle passed by on its way back. The lights inside were on, the radio blaring, and the peasants counted five bare-headed men. Later that night the van was left burning on the side of the road leading from the airport to La Libertad.

Around seven-thirty the following morning a peasant found the bodies of four North American women and an hour later, after identification by the local judge, they were buried in the dry earth of El Salvador.

It was not until the next day that their friends were told of the missionaries' death. Then, in the presence of the American Ambassador Robert White, the four bodies were exhumed. They were identified as Sisters Ita Ford and Maura Clarke, of the Maryknoll Sisters; Sister Dorothy Kazel, an Ursuline; and a tall blonde lay missioner in her twenties, Jeanie Donovan. Over the past few years I have several times watched the film of Jean Donovan's life, *Roses in December*, which shows the exhumation of these bodies. The shots are mercifully a little blurred, but one can still see clearly the limp figures in their jeans as they are hauled out of the grave with ropes. Time and again I have looked at Ita's body and thought *this* is what being a nun is about; this is about loving to the limit, about the grain of wheat falling to the ground and about the foolishness of those who follow Christ. There is a terrible purity in religious life when it is stripped of all the trappings of religion, of the self-consciousness, the elitism and the feeling of being holier than those in the world. I think of the girl in a lay institute who told me she would not wear a sleeveless dress because she thought of Jesus as her fiance and he would not like it; and of a friend, who after six years in a convent, felt "immodest" in trousers. There is no modesty in being found dead in a river in spate and none in being raped in the back of a van by a bunch of brutal security guards—just a foolish identification with the suffering of the world and with the Son of God made man. I find it very sad that Victorian prudery is confused with religious modesty and that the human body, its drives, and emotions are not understood for what they are: the creation of our all-loving, all-powerful God. Only when we are helped to love ourselves and our bodies, to know ourselves as fundamentally good, will we be able to start loving each other as the Lord commanded.

It occurs to me that I have been carried away by nostalgia, strayed a little from the theme. No matter. Perhaps the harsh sun of El Salvador has thrown light upon the deepest realities of caring, and the bleached bones of Ita Ford and Carla Piette remind us of the dust to which we must all return. Let me come back to the experience of community, but this time to my life with a group who, though nominally Christian, do not think of themselves as religious and who certainly have no call to celibacy: the staff of St. Luke's Hospice in Plymouth.

⋖ 13 ⋗

HOSPICE AS COMMUNITY

Have mercy on us Lord, have mercy.
You are the potter and we are the clay.
Somehow or other we have held together until now.
We are still carried by your mighty hand
and we are still clinging to your three fingers,
Faith, Hope and Charity
with which you support the whole great bulk of the earth,
that is to say, the whole weight of your people.
Cleanse our reins and hearts by the fire
of your holy spirit and establish the work
that you have wrought in us, lest we return
again to clay and nothingness.

William of St. Thierry
Twelfth-century Cistercian abbot of Rievaulx Abbey

It is only in the last year or so that I have come to see St.
Luke's Hospice as a community. Before that it was just the place
where I worked, a bit like the hospital but smaller and less
formal. Then one day I was listening to one of Jean Vanier's
tapes while driving my car and I heard a talk he had given to a
group of people who work in L'Arche. He spoke of people called
together because of their desire to serve a particular group of
the poor or disadvantaged and how what united them was not
the natural bonds of family, friendship, or common interest but
their calling to serve. This means that life in community will

almost always be difficult because such people have not chosen each other but have in a very real sense been *chosen* by their calling to serve.

I would not have *chosen* to live or work with many of my present "community" at St. Luke's and I doubt if many would have chosen me! We have been called together to work as a team because of our desire to work with the dying and our gifts to do that work. As in religious life, there are many who are inspired by the hospice ideal and would like to work in the field but find, when they try their "vocation," that the reality is very different from what they had imagined. Work with the dying requires not only great sensitivity and patience but a robust and earthy sense of humor for when you are in the business of caring for those whose bodies and minds are literally disintegrating, tragedy and farce are inexorably intertwined. There is too a deeply contemplative aspect to the work for it demands not just that we *do* things for people but that we *be* with them. It is a ministry of presence, a being alongside the suffering, impotent as they are impotent, mute as they are mute, sharing their darkness. As I described in an earlier chapter, this foot-of-the-cross ministry is enormously demanding because not only does it expose us to the pain of others, but it turns the spotlight upon our own weaknesses. The hardest thing for me about this work is not the contact with the patients and the exposure to their pain but my own recognition of the gulf between what I preach and what I practice. It is not so much that I teach a way of caring which I do not practice but that I can only sustain that level of caring for a limited period. There are days when I know I am working really well, that my sensitivity to people's pain and needs is finely tuned and I am using all my professional and spiritual skills. There are other days, however, when I find that I am distancing myself from the patients and their relatives, providing only the statutory level of physical care that ordinary medical practice requires. These are the days when I am tired or my mind is preoccupied or when I have just had enough and want out.

Most of the time, of course, one cannot take time out when one needs it or would like it. To be economically viable a caring service has to be organized in such a way that there is little overlap of staff, and that means that, unless one is really ill, one must press on as best one can, battle fatigued or not. This means that inevitably there will be days when people are irritable or bitchy and not only less sensitive to patients' needs, but less available to each other. I am personally acutely aware that I am not as friendly to junior nurses, domestic staff and volunteer helpers as I should be and not only do I appear distant, but sometimes, quite unwittingly, I hurt people. This is partly thoughtlessness but much more the fact that I have only a given amount of emotional energy to spend on being nice to people and sometimes, when I have spent a lot of this on patients, there is precious little left over for anyone else.

One of the lovely things about the hospice is the way in which we are learning to cope with each other's bad humor. In the early days there was a good deal of friction between various senior members of the staff, myself included. There were cliques and counter-cliques, jealousies and feuds and the occasional battle for supremacy. The ward office door was frequently closed and one could walk in upon what was clearly a private discussion about another member of staff. I was as guilty as anyone for I would flounce up to the office in a fury, shut the door and pour out my rage to one or another of the nurses. I know, in hindsight, that I was partly responsible for a good deal of the unrest at that time.

Conscious that all was not well between us and that stress levels were high, we made a number of attempts at "support groups" in which an outsider would meet with members of staff to discuss recent events and air any grievances. Both of the attempts foundered after a few weeks. In one group we met with a local clergyman who was experienced in working with junior hospital nurses. At first we would sit in silence and then someone would mention a recent "demanding" case and we would all agree that yes it had been very hard and we had found it very difficult. It took me a while to realize that these sessions were for me not only not helpful, but actually very frustrating. Here we were desperately dredging up problems in order to please the group facilitator who was generously giving up his time for us, and at the same time, quite unable to speak openly about the source of our pain.

It was not only he who was giving up his time, but those who were on duty were desperate to get back to their work while those who had come in during their off-duty were equally keen to escape. I felt particularly frustrated because I knew that we needed help and yet there was no way I could reveal to the junior nurses the feuds I was engaged upon with their seniors. Eventually the group foundered because too few people came and we all breathed a sigh of relief and reverted to our natural support strategies: letting off steam to the people whom *we* chose, when and where we felt like it!

Now, several years later, I can examine the situation with greater calm and observe where the *natural* support groups have formed. An important breakthrough for me personally, and I think for the hospice as a whole, was when I began to receive professional support outside the hospice. The fact of having an impartial skilled person to whom I could legitimately unload my anger and distress meant that I no longer wanted or needed to unburden inappropriately to the nurses or other members of staff.

One of the difficulties in a small unit is the loneliness of those in positions of responsibility. In a hospital the consultants can moan to each other about the ward nurses or the administrators, and vice versa, but in a small unit the head nurse, the doctor and the administrator are particularly alone, especially if they do not have a good working relationship with each other. I imagine it is the same in other specialties. I have gossiped to enough colleagues at hospice conferences over the last five years to know that interpersonal difficulties in management are almost par for the course. In some units the clash has been of such a magnitude that senior staff had to leave, and in some units head nurse, medical director, and administrator have all gone. This is not the place to go into the causes of conflict between these particular offices in the hospice movement, but it is worth noting that it exists, and that it is the cause of a huge burden of distress in dedicated professional people whose only conscious agenda is to relieve suffering.

In the five years that we have worked together a number of natural groupings and support strategies have emerged within our unit. One such grouping is those who have lunch together in the dining room. I should clarify this by saying that although in theory any member of staff is free to order a cooked lunch and eat it at the dining room table, in practice only a few senior staff do; the remainder, nurses and secretaries, prefer to carry soup and sandwiches off to their desks or wherever they can find to be alone with their peers. For the senior staff, however, head nurse, doctors, social worker and administrator, this meeting over the lunch table is vital daily communication. It is a time when we talk shop and let off steam, teasing, arguing and getting to know each other as people. It has been a rich experience for me to grow in love and respect for people for whom, at first, I had no natural affinity and to realize that they, like me, are a very human amalgam of strengths and frailties. It is not just a question of accepting others' frailties, but realizing that often these frailties are irrevocably bound up with who they are and therefore with their strengths and gifts. Humbling too has been the realization of how my own weaknesses are patiently accepted by the nursing and other staff because they, in their turn, value me not just for the work that I do, but for the person that I am.

The other very important grouping is those of us "on the frontline," those most closely involved with the patients. It has been a real delight for me to work with the same group of nurses over a period of six years. Without any facilitation or outside help we have bonded together as a team which functions as a single person. True, there are differences and friendships within the grouping, but there is a genuine respect for each other's expertise and personality that is quite special in the medical world. It is this teamwork which is the basis of hospice care, for no one person has the medical or personal resources to meet all the needs of any given patient. Out of the mutual respect there has flowered a genuine friendship between the members of the team so that we are able to share the darker side of our feelings about the work. This freedom to share is the essence of support, for if I feel "safe" enough in the group to admit that I feel badly about the way I have handled something or that I dislike a particular patient, then I open the way for others to speak of how they feel. It is in such circumstances that there emerges the most helpful and healing knowledge: that others also do things badly or become irritated by patients and their relatives, or feel guilty because they cannot give as much as they think they should.

This freedom to be yourself in the work situation is a very precious gift but, like all liberties, it must be respected and cherished. Where there is no such freedom, relationships are stilted and unsupportive, but where there is no respect for boundaries you have anarchy. Discovering where the boundaries lie in any given relationship takes time, and trust between people is something which must be earned, not demanded by right.

There is a fine balance, too, between how much personal distress should be shared in a work situation. An attempt to find this balance is important for two very different reasons. The first is that too great a degree of sharing of personal problems can lay an unfair burden upon other carers who are already under strain from an emotionally demanding job. It is one thing to reveal that one has a difficulty, another to talk about it repeatedly and at length. The second reason is one that I have learned to my cost: if those in positions of leadership reveal too much of their frailty, the people who depend on them may feel threatened and insecure. This has been for me one of the hardest things to bear in my present job. At the very time that I have been most in need of personal support—when I have been over-tired or anxious or depressed—I have had to struggle to keep a brave and serene face because if I did not, the word would be passed around that I "had problems" or could not cope and my job would be in jeopardy.

That I have found it necessary to keep up appearances in this way is, of course, a sign that relationships in the hospice are not perfect. But *of course* they are not perfect, for we are all wounded people and, as I wrote earlier, we are all groaning in a great travail as we are being fashioned into a community. It does, however, highlight a particular area of disharmony which I have found to be common in hospice circles and that is between the carers and their council of management. It may be that this disharmony is a characteristic of charities, a clash between dedicated lay and professional people with different visions or approaches to the same problem.

Perhaps it is worth exploring for a moment the causes of this friction for it is a major cause of distress for a number of senior hospice staff. Perhaps the first and simplest thing to say is that doctors and nurses do not like being told what to do by lay people! I certainly find myself bristling like a hedgehog when solicitors or business people or clergy appear to question the way I conduct my professional life. They in turn, I suspect, find themselves irritated beyond measure by what they perceive as the arrogance of clinicians who will not listen to advice from those with managerial skills.

One absurd but important cause of misunderstanding in my own situation has been a difference of vision between professionals and lay advisers of what the hospice should be doing. I do not doubt that similar problems exist in units for drug abuse, alcoholism or the care of the mentally handicapped. When the idea of a hospice for Plymouth was first conceived, a small nucleus of people dedicated themselves to making the dream a reality. They gave generously of their time and energy in meetings and fund-raising in order to set up a place where dying men and women would be cared for with love and skill. After five years their dream came true and their real problems began, for their "baby" took on a life and will of its own and began to develop in ways they had not bargained for. What had started life as a cozy ten-bed hospice where people would "die in dignity" became a bustling professional center whose members were called upon to visit patients in the community and in the hospital and to teach. The work of the hospice spread far beyond the four walls of its building and with this rapidly expanding endeavor came what those in business call "revenue consequences." A core staff which had been adequate in the early days became ever more thinly spread until they demanded that their numbers be increased. Another factor that the founders of the charity had not bargained for was that professionals who, in the early days of their dedication and enthusiasm, would work long hours for little money would not always be willing or able to keep up such a pace for months or years. I recall with some sadness the bitterness that I felt after nine months of my present job when I realized that my very considerable overtime work was not only not remunerated but not acknowledged.

How difficult it is for brothers and sisters to live in unity! In those early days, when I complained about my colleagues and managers, I was told that I must communicate better with them. This, at a time when we were barely on speaking terms, seemed like an impossible counsel of perfection. And now when I am able to live in relative peace with both peers and governors, I find myself giving exactly the same advice to colleagues who feel ill-used and misunderstood. But even as I say it, I see the same look in their eyes which says, "What me, talk to *them?* You must be joking, you just don't understand!"

Enough of division! Let us return to the idea of hospice as community and focus upon what our naval administrator calls the engine room: the people without whom the ship could not sail. One of the fascinating features of the hospice movement is what has come to be known as role overlap. This is just a jargon way of saying that where hierarchical barriers are not too rigid and a team is working well, different members will feel free to adapt to meet needs as they arise. It is not unusual in our situation to find the cook comforting grieving relatives, or the pastoral coordinator feeding a patient or sitting with someone who is restless. In the same way the secretary and receptionist in our front office provide warmth and a listening ear to the motley of visitors to the hospice. It is they who are the frontline of the endless droppers-in: the old ladies with their knitted knee blankets; the marathon runner with sponsor forms; and the shy, diffident widows and widowers who have plucked up courage to visit the hospice on the anniversary of the death of their spouse.

I am always fascinated by the ministry of these women in our front office and I hate to think of the nurse- or doctor-hours that would be needed to replace them if it was decreed that secretaries should confine themselves to typing and the taking of dictation.

And lastly, of course, are those who should be first in a hospice community, the patients. As in any community which cares for wounded people, they are the heart, the core, the reason for our existence. It is for them that we have come painfully together and they are the cement that binds us, despite our wounds and our "differences," into one body.

Like the carers, they bring their own gifts and wounds, their own idiosyncratic needs which we must strive to meet. Some ask no more of us than our kindness and our competence, a place of safety in our house. They are pilgrims, travelers who need a bed for a few nights before they continue their journey. Others, however, come yearning for love and acceptance, searching for a sense of belonging that has somehow eluded them. These are the people to whom we have something special to give: a renewed understanding of their worth as people, of their unique value as individuals. I am reminded today of a gentleman who was with us for a couple of weeks recently. I was asked to see him on the hematology ward where he was a patient. It had been decided that further treatment for his blood condition would not be in his best interests and that he would benefit from hospice care. At first he seemed a sad and rather pathetic figure, demoralized by his illness and unable to accept his impending death. During the course of our conversation he spoke wistfully of his home and of his electric organ, which he knew he would never play again. Gambling on the goodwill of the head nurse and the administrator at St. Luke's, I said that this was nonsense and that he must come *with* his organ and play it for us. Never will I forget the way that man's face changed. When he realized that I was serious, his eyes lit up and he seemed to sit straighter and taller. From being useless, he was suddenly wanted again, his sense of dignity restored. Two days later he came to us and the day after that the administrator went home with him to collect the organ in the hospice van. It was only a week or so that he was well enough to play for us, but those days could have been a lifetime for the joy they brought him. It is a rare happiness and privilege for us to provide a home and family for people such as this and reward enough when they mutter in disbelief, "I never knew places like this existed."

A TIME OF THE OLIVE PRESS

It is a time of fear, of apprehension,
a fear of pain and disfigurement,
a fear of hateful eyes and deeds of violence,
a fear of the power of those who want
to quarantine, to imprison,
to tattoo with identity marks
(shades of Auschwitz),
a fear of the death dealing.
There is a tightening,
a pressure on the chest,
a desire for air, for space
beyond the narrow constricted gate.
There is cold fear in a time of tribulation,
a time of the olive press, the wine press,
the crushing of grapes,
and no guarantee of a good vintage.

Jim Cotter
from *Healing More or Less*

It happens from time to time that people ask me if I will stay in Plymouth or go somewhere else, perhaps even return to Chile. I usually smile and say I don't really know; but I have no immediate plans to move on. It is difficult to explain that working day by day with the dying makes one acutely conscious that life is a gift and one cannot count on receiving it tomorrow, let alone in a year's time. At a more personal level, I have a deep sense of having been chosen to do this work and I remain ever open to the possibility that I might burn-out or be sent somewhere else. Like many people, I wonder very much if the present AIDS epidemic will change my life, if we at the hospice will be drawn into caring for a quite different group of dying people. This chapter is a reflection, a viewpoint from someone waiting in the wings, not knowing when, or even if, their name will be called.

It is May 1987, and I sit at my desk watching the ships on Plymouth Sound. The supply ship lies patiently at anchor by the breakwater, dull and grey in the afternoon light, awaiting the transforming darkness when she will be lit up like an ocean liner, casting magical reflections on the black water. A white yacht, a blue spinnaker filled with wind, races across the bow of a shabby rust-colored tanker while the pleasure cruiser takes yet another load of sightseers up the Hamoaze to get a glimpse of the warships lying quietly at anchor, waiting for refit. The dockyard and its ships are an integral part of Plymouth, providing work for its menfolk; and for us at the hospice a steady trickle of "mesos" — mesotheliomas, the lethal asbestos-related lung cancers, which catch a man unawares, twenty or thirty years after he has been exposed to the dust. And somewhere, scattered secretly throughout the city, are thirty men whose blood tests show they are infected with the AIDS virus. What are *they* doing, I wonder, this grey Saturday afternoon? Are they milling around the city center with the other lads, happily anonymous — or sitting in bed, waiting, wondering, terrified and alone? I remember Jim Cotter's poem, written for an evening of meditation in San Francisco and my heart goes out to the lonely and afraid:

> There is cold fear in a time of tribulation,
> a time of the olive press, the wine press,
> the crushing of grapes,
> and no guarantee of a good vintage.

This chapter, like all the others, can only be written from where I sit, this day, in the spring of 1987. It will be a little out of date next week and surely more distant when this book is published. And yet it must be written, must have its own validity as a stage on a journey into an unknown tomorrow. For me, the future with AIDS is a particularly unknown quantity. With thirty men HIV positive today, it is predicted there will be two or three who will be dying of AIDS in two years time. Perhaps, though, there will be many more and we shall need a special hospice, and a team of people to care for them. I do not know yet if I will be involved, but as a doctor specializing in terminal care, it seems likely.

What will it be like, I wonder? How will we cope? Will it bring a whole new series of demands that we long to live up to but cannot? I, too, am a little afraid, not of the idea of contagion — that is no longer a nightmare — but at the idea of being caught up in a tidal wave of anguish that will roll me over and over until I am disorientated and gasping for breath.

Again rises from the heart of suffering the ancient
    cry,
O God, why? O God, how long?
And the cry is met with silence.
Dare I look steadily at Christ,
at God involved in the isolation and despair,
willing to be contaminated, to be infected,
loving faithfully and in patient endurance,
until all that is being created reaches its final destiny,
in glory, joy and love?
And yet, why *this* degree of pain?
Why these ever-repeated battles,
with a swathe cut through a generation?
Horrific sacrifice — for what?
Why? Why?

Jim Cotter
from *Healing More or Less*

The *Brittany* ferry ploughs a grey furrow across the Sound, scattering the sailing boats like so many barnyard chickens. The door in its broad stern is tightly shut, grim-lipped in defiance against the waves and the memory of the *Herald of Free Enterprise* in which so many died in the cold waters off Zeebrugge. Why? why? we all cried, as we sat glued to radio and television, aghast at the waste of life and the thought that "there by the grace of God go I." The anguished "why" of the dying is never more poignant than in the young, and those who love them. How will we cope with this when it is compounded by fear of contagion, social ostracism and guilt? The young dying of cancer frequently become honored in their community; people rally round, money is raised in pubs and schools for treatment in America or at least a holiday in Majorca. But AIDS. Who will come and sit with *these* patients? Who will stand in church and pray for them by name? Who will hold their frightened hands or cradle in their arms a frail, sore-covered body racked with the sobs of intolerable grief. Jim Cotter writes:

> AIDS shows up clearly what our attitudes are.
> It is forcing us to choose,
> and the degree of our health is revealed by our
>   response.

Do we punish those who suffer, compounding their suffering by condemnation and social ostracism, withdrawal of insurance, and graffiti on the wall? Or do we go out and meet them in their heartache and distress? Do we quote passages from the story of Sodom and Gomorrah to substantiate our unconscious fears — or remember that Jesus was the man who touched lepers and refused to condemn the woman taken in adultery? How tempting it is to oversimplify the moral issues involved, rather than being open to a culture different from our own. How tempting, too, to agree that compulsory testing and quarantine are the answer, forgetting that the sick are beloved of God and are our brothers and sisters.

It seems to me that the AIDS epidemic is offering the single largest and most clear-cut challenge to the Christian community of this decade, if not this century. The demands are made, the gauntlet thrown down at the whole of society, but it is we Christians who *claim* to follow the God made man who loved and healed the unclean. The gospels are unequivocal in their teaching:

> Be compassionate as your Father is compassionate. Do not judge, and you will not be judged yourselves; do not con-

demn, and you will not be condemned yourselves; grant pardon, and you will be pardoned. Give, and there will be gifts for you: a full measure, pressed down, shaken together, and running over, will be poured into your lap; because the amount you measure out is the amount you will be given back. (Luke 6:36-38)

In many places, Christians are prominent in the community's response to the distress of AIDS sufferers, but in others they are open in their condemnation. Some priests and pastors are quick to condemn the secular "play safe" approach to prevention, but give no exhortation from the pulpit to understand, to befriend, to forgive.

How easy it is to be selective in our understanding of the gospels, to get hung up on sexual morality and lose sight of the message of compassion and forgiveness. Even easier is the subconscious decision that this is someone else's problem and no concern of ours, so that we find ourselves hurrying busily by on the other side of the road. For me, for my team at the hospice, this time of decision is yet to come. Already we are saying openly among ourselves that we will take AIDS cases—but in the same breath we mutter, "What will the other patients say?" How will the ordinary patients and their families cope with the knowledge that the patient down the corridor has AIDS? They need not know, people say: confidentiality must be maintained. But will that really be possible, especially if many members of the gay community are involved? Perhaps it will be easier to care for people at home; but how will the ladies from the meals-on-wheels service manage, and how will the district nurse be greeted when she comes from the AIDS patient to the mother with a new baby? Of course we do not know how things will be, but we foresee much heartache and difficulty.

Then of course there is the inevitable gulf between theory and reality. Sometimes it happens that we do not have the emotional resources to cope with very difficult, wounded patients. It is difficult to go on loving someone who is manipulating or who is cruel to other patients. So often it is the very poor one longs to love but cannot quite manage to. There have been too many hurts to establish a good and trusting relationship in a short time and one can only do one's best, always acutely conscious of a sense of failure and what might have been. Such situations are enormously draining—yet good for the humility! We get so much affirmation that we are in danger of believing that we are indeed angels in disguise.

Meanwhile we wait, with the rest of England, with an eye to San Francisco, Zaire and the reports from our own capital cities. Perhaps the cure will be found before the epidemic hits Plymouth, but if it is not, we pray that we may not be found wanting.

⊰ 15 ⊱

DISCIPLES ALONE

If you live alone,
whose feet will you wash?
St. Basil the Great
Fourth century

In the early days of my Christian searching there appeared to be two basic options: to be married or to become a member of a religious community. No one spoke to me of a third option: that I might simply remain as I was, a single woman. Even now in these more lay-conscious times it seems that little has been worked out in the way of spirituality for those who either consciously choose not to marry or find that the single life has somehow chosen them. I am not talking here specifically of those who feel called to a life of celibacy but to the wider body of individuals who find themselves, for whatever reason, alone.

People live alone for many reasons. Some make a positive decision for a life of celibacy and take public or private vows. Some are divorced, some widowed or deserted, and others find that marriage just never came their way or that they did not particularly want to share their lives with another person. Whatever the reason for their single status, such people, men or women, must find a *modus vivendi* that works for them, in which they can be well and happy and fruitful. In this chapter I would like to explore some of my own experience of discipleship lived alone in the hope that it may be relevant for others.

I did not set out to live alone. Indeed for many years, like most young women, I assumed that I would marry and live happily ever after. Then, in my teens, I felt a calling to the religious life and for the next twenty years or so I played a sort of hide and seek game with what I thought of as the Hound of Heaven. Eventually, in my early forties, I made my *fiat* and with a massive leap of faith entered a monastic community of women. Eighteen months later I was again in the world, psychologically quite battered and very clear that I had no vocation to be a nun. It was not that I had "lost" my vocation through carelessness or infidelity, just that religious life in community was not for me. So what then? What do you do when the Carthusian monk inside you has tried to give away everything to follow Christ and then crawled back bleeding and in tears? What do you do with the story of Jesus and the rich young man which has inspired and tormented you for most of your lifetime? Do you decide that the call to sell all is directed at someone else—or do you try and live it out wherever you happen to be, clinging to the call of the radical gospel with a grim determination and bleeding, broken fingernails?

When I was on my way out of the convent in 1980 I spent a couple of nights at Stanbrook Abbey, a large Benedictine monastery where I know a number of the nuns. The then-abbess, a tall and regal lady, came up to me in the refectory and, towering above me, said in her best abbatial tones, "Sheila, *what* have you been doing?" Nonplussed, I muttered that I had been trying to fit myself like a square peg into a round hole. She paused, thoughtful, for a moment and then, with devastating simplicity, said, "Why don't you just be Sheila?"

I was too battered and sick at heart then to laugh or realize the depth of her wisdom but I have spent the last seven years doing just that and I commend it as a rule of life for all who find themselves exhausted and bewildered in their search to do God's will. As another monastic friend put it to me, "The great moment of take-off comes when we stop trying to do God's will and allow his will to be done in us."

But just being Sheila was not something I learned to do overnight nor will you learn to be Mary or Michael or whoever in the twinkling of an eye. Discovering who one is and how one is meant to live and be seem to take a lifetime of trial and error, laughter and tears. In those early post-convent days I still wanted to be a cross between Joan of Arc, Michael Hollings, and Helder Camara, and I set out to live my life accordingly. For a little while I tried to be a hermit, living in a trailer on my brother's farm, but it was not long before penury drove me back to the only work I know: being a doctor.

Having rediscovered, to my surprise, that this was my true vocation I set out to live the demands of the radical Gospel as a resident in a Plymouth hospital. The first thing I knew with great clarity was that I must never own property again. Having given away my house in Chile and sold my Devon home to give the money to the poor I was determined not to be shackled by possessions yet again. I would live in the hospital residency, keep a little of my salary for pocket money and give the rest away to feed the starving of the Third World.

This lasted about three weeks until I made a friend and wanted to ask her to stay for the weekend. Even radical disciples must have someone to play with, I reasoned, but where was she going to sleep? On the floor of your room, you might reasonably answer, but I was forty-four not twenty, and a fretful sleeper at the best of times. That time I was able to borrow a room from the hospital but I realized that if I was to have any kind of social life, I must move out of the hospital and find somewhere to live. For the next few weeks I searched for an apartment to rent. Not a large apartment, of course, just a small home where I could live the simple life and have friends of like mind to stay. The trouble with apartments, I discovered, was that there were very few to rent unfurnished and those with furniture were both expensive and decorated in a style which did not particularly appeal to me. I was bemoaning this fact to one of my colleagues, a man twenty years my junior, when he said to me in an exasperated voice, "But why don't you *buy* an apartment, like the rest of us? The mortgage payments work out cheaper than the rent."

So much for my ambition not to own property! I took his advice and set out to buy an apartment. It would be a small one, inexpensive so that I would still be in solidarity with the poor (well, the moderately poor!). But of course the simple life does not come naturally to middle-aged, middle-class doctors and when I contemplated buying an apartment in one of the poorer areas of town the nurses laughed at me and said, "Don't be stupid. You wouldn't be safe to walk in the street at night down there." Then one day the real estate agent phoned and said, "Doctor Cassidy, we've found your apartment!" And so he had: it was an attic apartment overlooking the sea in a nice safe part of town, so I got a mortgage and moved in to live happily ever after.

But the Helder Camara in me was not yet ready to give way to the real Sheila. Determined to be *seen* to be poor I vowed to furnish the place entirely with second-hand things and leave the floors spartanly bare. That was the winter my back went and I spent many agonizing moments on my knees trying to sweep the bare stairs with a dust pan and brush. Eventually I gave in and had the place carpeted and bought a vacuum cleaner so that I did not have to bend down. But if a vacuum cleaner was a justifiable necessity, a washing machine certainly was not. I would wash my clothes by hand, trampling the sheets and towels underfoot in the bath like the peasants or some crazy monk friends of mine! All that summer my clothes got greyer and greyer until I could bear it no longer and gave a pile of towels and shirts to my cleaning lady to wash at home. (I should have added that somewhere along the way I had acquired a cleaning lady: if I could not be in solidarity with the poor, at least I could give them work!) It took only three weeks for me to calculate that the two pounds a week that I was paying to have shirts and two towels washed would be more intelligently spent on weekly payments on a washing machine, so the next Saturday afternoon I abandoned the simple life and bought one.

Perhaps the final fall from my self-styled perch of grace came at the beginning of the winter season when *Brideshead Revisited* was serialized for television. Until then I had stalwartly refused to have more than a transistor radio and tape recorder, but now I could bear it no longer and rushed into town to buy myself a TV.

What then is the lesson to be learned from this "failure" to live the simple life? I am hesitant to pontificate lest I be accused of justifying my weakness and self-indulgence. I can only observe that each step I made toward the norm for the people among whom I lived left me a little less arrogant and a little less pleased with myself. As the years have passed I have become less rather than more sure of what it means to follow the gospel demands in the middle of a materialist society. What I am quite clear about, however, is that my place, at this moment, is to be planted right in the middle of that society. And the great joke is that the more I get to know the ordinary people who inhabit this wicked materialist world the more I am amazed by their generosity and goodness. They may have washing machines and hi-fis, videos and color television but they are often more loving and compassionate and forgiving than those whose energies are consumed with living the simple life. The older I get the less I know except that the one thing that really matters is loving. The really disconcerting thing for Christians is when they meet non-believers who are more honest, more generous and more loving than they are. It happened to me in prison in Chile and it happens to me every day now in Plymouth. As I have remarked before, the Spirit of God blows where it wills and we Christians have no monopoly on goodness.

As the years go by I become more and more convinced of the truth of the Abbess of Stanbrook's advice and I have learned to be more gentle with myself. On the notice board in my bedroom I have a postcard which depicts a fat, yellow, lion-like beast having spots patiently stuck all over his coat: spots that will surely come unstuck in the first shower of rain. For years I have tried to be something that I am not and it just does not work. I, who would like to be tall and thin, naturally ascetic and intellectual, am short and a bit plump and like watching television and reading whodunits. I would like to be the sort of person who unwinds from the day's work by listening to classical music—but I do not. I do it by gossiping on the phone or watching TV. I would like to be tidy and content with few possessions—but I am extremely messy and acquire an inordinate amount of clutter! Little by little, though, I am coming to appreciate the Sheila that God made and be content with my gifts and personality. It does not mean that I do not struggle to overcome my frailties but that I am less disheartened by my failures than I used to be.

This learning to understand ourselves and being patient with
our needs and frailties is particularly important for people who
live alone. If I do not have a husband to cherish me and protect
me from doing too much I must learn to look after myself. It is
not just a question of eating sensibly and going to bed at midnight but of learning where my limits are and what lifts me when
I am down. I have to give myself permission to say no to requests
I cannot handle and to take time out when I need it. To put it
bluntly, when you live alone you have a responsibility to take
care of yourself because no one else will and you are no use to
anyone if you burn out before your time! It is not only illogical
but arrogant to think that we are exempt from the common
human need for rest, for fun and for time out.

How you reconcile your own needs with the poverty and
anguish of the Third World is a question of experimentation and
balance. There are, I believe, two basic concepts which can
inform our thinking and guide our decision-making. The first is
the concept of global family. This says that we are all children
of the same God, with the same rights to food, shelter, work and
freedom. This means that we must care about injustice and poverty and the threat of nuclear war. How we express that caring
will depend upon our gifts and resources at any given moment.

The second concept is that of the stewardship of resources.
This means that I am a steward, not an owner of my health, my
intelligence, my gifts, and my possessions. If my gifts enable me
to earn more than I need, then I must share what I have with
those who are less gifted. Just how I live out this philosophy will
depend upon my strength and courage at any given moment. As
in other areas in which I preach there is a massive gulf between
theory and practice, but basically it means that I try to find what
I need to be well and happy and stick to that. It means that I
am not always aiming for a bigger and better house or car or
record player but am content with what I have and it also means
that I am happy to share my possessions with those around me.
I do not pretend that this is radical gospel living but it is what
I can manage here and now. There is no doubt that I have more
possessions now than the day I came out of the convent but I
hope too that I have more understanding of the frailty of ordinary people.

Another area in which we must know ourselves is that of our *emotional* needs. It has taken me many years and a good deal of professional assistance to undo the conditioning of a puritanical religious upbringing in which I was taught to be ashamed of my body and my longing for warmth and affection. It is a great joy to me now to know myself known and loved by the God who made me and to understand that all that I feel and am is God's work. It is not my intention to write down an answer to the inevitable question of "How far can you go?" but simply to say that I am grateful to those who have taught me to accept my sexuality as God-given and intrinsically good.

There remains of course a gulf between the *acknowledgement* of oneself as a normal human being yearning for love and affection and the meeting of those needs. In this area I am far from having all the answers but I share with you what I believe to be one very important insight: if you fill every day, every evening and every weekend with work, then you will crowd out the space that is essential for being with friends and being peaceably on your own. It is so easy, if one is single, to work during the day and get caught up in meetings, conferences and good works in the evenings and weekends so that when one does suddenly find the evening is free there is a devastating void and sense of loneliness that leaves one feeling worthless, stupid and unloved.

I recall some years ago when I was working full-time in medicine and doing human rights lecturing or preaching most weekends that I sought the help of a psychologist in the belief that he would help me organize myself to be more productive. I thought that with a little expert advice I would be able to cram even more into my life. I sent him an enormous and complex timetable of my life and other engagements of the past three years, color coded to show whether they were national or local, human rights or religious, and so on. I do not know if I had expected him to compliment me on my energy or my good works but he looked me straight in the eye and said, with a lovely Scottish accent, "Thank you for sending me your material; I've read it carefully and I'm appalled."

Perhaps the Scots articulate the word "appalled" in a special way, but his comment went home and I listened with unwonted attention and humility while he explained to me that I was destroying myself with overwork and a lifestyle which denied most of my ordinary human needs for rest, friendship, and recreation. It has taken a very long time to unscramble the mess that I was so proud of, and I am still very vulnerable to overstretching myself, but I am now much healthier and less lonely than I was a couple of years ago. Slowly I am learning that the cure for loneliness is not to be away from home every weekend but to make quite sure that I am not away too much. One must learn to love one's home and be at peace in it for otherwise one is without an anchor and at the mercy of every wave and undercurrent.

I still do not fully understand the psychology of women and their homes but I believe that there is a deep connection between the place one lives in and the person one is. Like one's clothes it becomes an extension of oneself, a means of expressing who one is. I have come to love my home so that, like Mole in *The Wind in the Willows*, whiskers twitch at the thought of it when I have been away too long. The cheap purple carpet that I found in my bedroom when I bought the place has long since gone and I have spent more money than I would have once thought proper upon alterations, decorating, and furnishing. Perhaps I have fallen so far from grace that I have lost sight of my original gospel ideals. I do not know. But what I do know is that for a number of years I have been involved in a demanding ministry of healing the sick and preaching the gospel and I have now worked out a way of life that works for me, a *modus vivendi* in which I can be well and happy and in which my various gifts are being used creatively for others.

I like to think that, although I am once more a woman of many possessions, I cling to them less fiercely than before and that I use them in accordance with the rule of thumb laid down by Ignatius of Loyola in his Principle and Foundation:

Man is created to praise, reverence, and serve God our Lord, and by this means to save his soul.

All the other things on the face of the earth are created for man to help him in attaining the end for which he is created.

Hence, man is to make use of them in as far as they

help him in the attainment of his end, and he must rid himself of them in as far as they prove a hindrance to him.

Therefore we must make ourselves indifferent to all created things, as far as we are allowed free choice and are not under any prohibition. Consequently, as far as we are concerned, we should not prefer health to sickness, riches to poverty, honor to dishonor, a long life to a short life. The same holds for all things.

Our one desire and choice should be what is more conducive to the end for which we are created. (*Spiritual Exercises*)

⊰{ 16 }⊱

PRAYING ALONE

Prayer and work
are not whole without each other.
"Rule for a New Brother"
Blessed Sacrament Fathers
Brackkenstein Community,
Holland

If there is one thing, one belief that Christian carers have in common, it is the conviction that they don't pray enough! The majority of men and women, in vows or not, who are struggling to live their lives according to the demands of the gospel are convinced of the need for prayer—but they find it very difficult to carry this conviction into practice. I should say at the outset that I do not think I pray enough either, but at least this gives me some insight into the problems.

What are the difficulties, then, in combining a ministry of caring with a life of prayer—is it even possible? Should those of us who feel called to a deep relationship with God in prayer lay down our tools and make for the nearest Carmelite or Benedictine monastery? Many of us do, of course, and emerge bruised and perplexed, one, five or even twenty years later. Some have the good sense to know without trying the life that they could not survive cooped up in a convent, but perhaps they decide that, since they have no calling to the religious life they can have no calling to prayer.

I believe that one of the problems in helping people to combine a life of prayer with an active apostolate is a purely semantic issue: the meaning of the word contemplative. In modern religious parlance, there are two broad categories of religious life: the *active* and the *contemplative.* Those men and women called to the active life involve themselves in such activities as nursing or teaching or other pastoral activities. They are expected to say their prayers night and morning and get on with their work in between. No one expects of them that they will become mystics or contemplatives; they are the Marthas, the busy ones whose job it is to wash feet, to serve. The contemplative life, we are brought up to believe, is for those with a special vocation for prayer, with a higher calling. These are the Marys, those who have "chosen the better part." They must leave "the world" to its own devices, withdrawing from its pleasures, distractions, and demands so that they can devote their life wholly to God. These are the monastic men and women, the Carmelites, the Cistercians and the Benedictines: those who would embrace the dry martyrdom of renunciation, and who are truly fools for Christ.

I believe that this division into the "active" and the "contemplative" life is not only simplistic, but inaccurate. I believe, furthermore, that it is actually quite dangerous, for people with a desire for prayer but unfitted for the *enclosed* life find themselves in convents where they are ill at ease and unhappy. Such men or women, knowing that they are called to a life of prayer, may enter monastery after monastery, only to leave each one emotionally wounded and with an ever-deepening sense of failure. Others who never even make it into the cloisters spend their lives looking wistfully through the wrong side of the grille, wishing they too had a "vocation" to be a contemplative.

The truth is, of course, that while a few people are indeed both attracted and suited to the enclosed religious life, the vast majority of us must live out our discipleship in the wider community, marrying for better or for worse, rearing our children and earning our living as best we may. But though only a minority of people are called to the *enclosed* life of the monk or nun, a great many find themselves drawn to a life of contemplative prayer. That is why it is so important that we do not use the words *enclosed* and *contemplative* interchangeably, for while it is true that some men and women find that their contemplative prayer flowers in the desert of the monastery, others will grow *only* in the midst of society, in the marketplace. If a man or woman experiences that indefinable hunger for God and for prayer that are the signs of a contemplative vocation they must discern, *not* whether or not they have a calling *to* prayer, but *where*, desert or marketplace, they should live out that calling.

To some people there is great mystery and grace about the monastic life: a mystery heightened by the beauty of the liturgy and the medieval clothes worn by monks and nuns. Even now, when I have spent eighteen months on the "inside," my heart thrills to the sound of the Gregorian chant and the sight of black cowled or veiled figures gliding down a bare cloister. I remember with deep nostalgia the stillness after Compline at Stanbrook or the peal of the Ampleforth bell announcing the Grand Silence. My memories of the eighteen months I spent as a real nun, rather than a make-believe one, are infinitely less romantic, but even so I recall the peace that comes with a life which is deeply caught up in the rhythms of the liturgy and in which silence plays an integral part.

Why, then, did I not stay? The answer is simple: I am not temperamentally suited to the enclosed life. I need contact with other people to remain healthy and outward-looking; I need to serve. So what of us failed monks, the contemplatives manqués who lust for the choral office, the Grand Silence and Lectio Divina in a sunlit corner of the cloister? Should we admit our second-best status as Marthas or work out a way in which we can have the best of both worlds? For me it is the "apostolic" spirituality of Ignatius of Loyola which best meets my needs, for it is a way of being in which prayer and action are not compartmentalized but inexorably interwoven and in which, ideally, action springs *from* contemplation. It is a way of living out the gospel which sees God in all things: in the kitchen, in the marketplace, in anguish and in peace. God is at work in the universe and in creatures, laboring and loving, shaping and molding like the great potter of the monk William: "You are the potter, we are the clay."

Spirituality is about living with, in, and for God, and the great spiritualities of the church are just the ways in which different personalities have found their own idiosyncratic way to God. We may have found that one particular way suits us to a tee or we may be eclectic, making for ourselves a mongrel way which is, for us, the way of the Lord. Ignatius was a soldier and he brings to the church the way of an inner discipline. Misunderstood, his way can seem rigid and stultifying; read aright it gives a great freedom from the heart. You get the best feel of Ignatius in his Principle and Foundation (quoted above). He states quite simply the reason for our existence: we are to praise, revere and serve the Lord our God. Everything else is to help us do just that. So time and money, food and clothes, work and leisure are all to be used or discarded insofar as they help us attain the end for which we are created.

It is a marvelously flexible, adaptable philosophy, stunning in its simplicity and ruthless in its single-mindedness. In particular it is a way which is not hung up on rituals, lifestyle, or ways of dressing. If dressing up in the garb of a fifteenth-century widow helps you to serve God, Ignatius is saying, go for it. If you find it gets in the way, see how you get on in jeans; but do not kid yourself that one outfit is holier than the other. Of course he did not actually say that, but I like to think he might have if he lived today.

"I will enter upon the meditation, now kneeling, now prostrate on the ground, now lying face upwards, now seated, now standing, always being intent on seeking what I desire" (*Spiritual Exercises*, no. 76). If my extrapolation from number 76 in the Exercises is taking a little liberty with Ignatius, it gives us an opportunity to dwell upon the spirit and wisdom of what he is saying about personal prayer. Another way of putting it would be in the words of the Benedictine abbot John Chapman who wrote with marvelous English simplicity, "Pray as you can and not as you can't." If the rosary is your thing, say it and love it, but if it screws you up to repeat the Hail Mary fifty times in ten minutes, do not feel guilty; find out what *does* suit you and stick to it. If you feel comfortable praying crosslegged on the floor with a candle and an icon, lovely; but do not be surprised if your charismatic friends want to sit in a circle singing in tongues or your Irish auntie has to go to church to say the Stations of the

Cross. In the Father's house there are many mansions — if it was
not so, he would have told us. In the human race there are many
cultures and many tastes and we must let people pray in the way
that is right for them, and hope that they will let us do the same.

This respect for our neighbor must be carried inward as
respect for our own heart because what is good for us one day
will not necessarily be right for every day. There is a great art
in learning to pray with your inclinations rather than doggedly
against them:

> Your prayer will take countless forms
> because it is the echo of your life,
> and a reflection of the inexhaustible light
> in which God dwells.
>   "Rule for a New Brother"

Perhaps then, it is worth looking at a few of the different
ways in which we can pray. I would dare to say that no one is
superior or preferable to the other; it is a question of what is
given to you, of what you are able. The first way we learn to
pray is with words: words taught us by our parents or guardi-
ans — God bless Mummy and Daddy or the Our Father. These
early prayers may stay with us until we are grey haired so that
we wake with a muttered:

> My God I offer to you this day
> All I shall think or do or say . . .

Using other people's words is something that most people do
some of the time. Which words we use does not seem to matter
a lot to me (except insofar as they may reveal that our theology
is a bit rocky!). For some of us the Psalms will be food and
drink, for others the Book of Common Prayer or other set
prayers. Sometimes we will dwell upon the words, at other times
we will barely notice them, using them almost as a mantra to
still our restless hearts or as a magic carpet carrying our unspoken longing to God.

At other times, set words will pall and our own phrases well
up from the heart. "Lord, help me. I'm so bloody miserable.

What on earth am I going to do?" We should always feel free to pray whatever words are in our hearts, for what manner of a God would reject the cries of his child?

Sometimes, of course, we need no words. Our hearts swell with an inarticulate longing or are somehow silenced so that no words are necessary. Then we should just sit in silence, longing, hurting, loving, or bored, just being in the presence of the one who made us.

These are all respectable, well-recognized ways of praying but there is nothing to stop us inventing our own. I love to pray on the beach in the early morning and will walk along the very edge of the sea singing whatever psalm is in my head to no particular tune and in no known harmony. Other times I take a stick or my toes and write I LOVE YOU in enormous letters in the sand—leaving it to the tide to wash it away or some bemused dog-walker to wonder what crazy lovers have been cavorting in the waves.

One thing which I think stops a lot of people from praying is a lack of understanding of what Ignatius calls *consolation* and *desolation*. Consolation (with sun) is the term used to describe those positive feelings of faith, hope, and love. It is an overflowing of the desire for God into the feelings. It is a pleasant experience, but one which we must not count upon because anyone who prays regularly will experience boredom and dryness, not through lack of love, but for many different, sometimes quite mundane reasons. It is important to hold in mind that prayer is an act of the will and if we make time to attend to God, then we are praying, even if all we feel is our fatigue, our rumbling stomach or the myriad distractions that overrun our conscious minds. Desolation (without sun), in Ignatius's language is negative feeling in relation to God and his will. It may be the result of depression or fatigue or perhaps some conflict between our different needs and desires. But whether our prayer be characterized by consolation or by dryness and turmoil, what matters is that we should pray and keep on praying.

Here it is worth speaking of discipline in the spiritual life. Those who choose and can adapt to life in a monastery have one great advantage: their whole life is structured and geared to the liturgy. The bell wakes them from sleep and they go to church and so on, throughout the day. Those of us in the world, however, must devise our own framework or prayer will be rapidly squeezed out of life by work or other demands. Each of us must find a routine that fits with his temperament and lifestyle, and it must be a routine that works, not an impossible counsel of perfection. It matters little how we organize ourselves, just that we do it. Some people will find it easier to make time in the morning, others the evening and some in the middle of the day. For me the morning is the easiest time and I pray for about half an hour each day when I wake up. There are days when I can pray in the evening too, but often I am too tired and restless to settle down. There are two points to make here. The first is that, the more you pray, the more you will find that you want to pray. If you establish a daily routine of prayer, missing it will become almost impossible because there will be a hunger for it, a sense of something missing. Conversely, the less you pray the less you will want to pray and the more impossible it will seem to make time. The other thing is that if you make time for prayer in a regular disciplined way, there will be a great spin-off because prayer will start to overflow into the rest of your life so that you will find yourself praying at the bus stop, driving the car, or while watching television. In the same way that thoughts of the beloved will crowd into the lover's consciousness, so thoughts of God will come easily in and out of the mind of the person who is faithful in prayer.

Discipline in prayer and in one's way of living leads in time to real freedom of spirit so that one learns to adapt quite unconsciously to one's own and other people's needs. Ignatius is quite clear on this, telling his disciples that, if the demands of charity take them away from their time of prayer, they are not the less acceptable to God. The apostolic life is like a journey in the desert—you may have to travel for quite a while on what is in the camel's hump—but when the time of rest at the oasis comes, one drinks long and deep at the well to recharge the batteries and prepare for the next journey. Like many apostolic people, I have found that there is a very special sweetness in prayer after a period of apostolic activity, for one moves from preaching or whatever into deep stillness and consolation. It is not a question of work *or* prayer but of a life in which the two are inexorably welded together, prayer giving one power to serve and generous foot-washing leading to sweetness at rest in the presence of God. It is in this way that St. Paul's amazing admonition to pray always can literally be obeyed, and there comes a time when one dares to say with him, "I live now, not I but Christ lives in me" (Gal. 2:20).

⊰ 17 ⊱

DISCIPLESHIP AS LISTENING

Eli said to Samuel, "Go and lie down, and if someone calls say, 'Speak, Yahweh, your servant is listening.' " So Samuel went and lay down in his place. (1 Sam. 3:9)

The key to discipleship is listening and if we are to take seriously the call to follow Christ we must listen to what he is asking of us. Men and women in religious life commonly take vows of poverty, chastity, and obedience and those of us who are not thus committed are tempted to breathe a sigh of relief and thank our lucky stars that we are not tied down. If we reflect upon it, however, there is a sense in which all Christians are bound with Hosea's leading reins of love:

> I led them with reins of kindness,
> with leading strings of love.
> Hos. 11:4

Christ demands quite clearly of all of us that we share our wealth with our brothers and sisters, that we be chaste of heart and that we listen to his voice. Again and again in the gospels he calls us to listen: "I am the way, the truth and the life"; "I am the Bread of Life"; "He who hears me hears the Father"; "Come to me all you who are heavily laden and I will give you rest."

How then can we be so obtuse as to think that it is only the professed religious who are bound by vows of obedience — for the word obedience comes from the root *audire*, to hear — and obedience in its essence is listening. How then should lay Christians listen to the word of God and in particular, how should those of us involved in caring cash out our "obedience"? I would suggest six areas of life in which we must be particularly sensitive, tuned in to hear what God is asking of us. The first of these (and I do not set them in any order of importance) is scripture. There are many people for whom daily reading of the Bible is as natural as having breakfast or brushing their teeth, but for others less well-disciplined it is a struggle to be faithful. One of the great bonuses of the monastic life for me was the daily exposure of the "Wild Word of God," that word which both warms the heart and pierces it, slipping as St. Paul says, into the secret places of the heart, between the joints of the marrow.

There are many different ways of reading the Bible. You can read a whole gospel through at a sitting or get stuck in wonder over a paragraph or a single phrase. The old monks in their Lectio Divina read slowly, pondering, chewing and ruminating on small passages so that they could extract from them the power contained in the poetry. I personally find it absurdly difficult to be disciplined about daily scripture reading but find that fidelity to saying even part of the Divine Office provides me with at least some exposure.

The second of my channels of the word of God is what I would loosely call the church — by which I mean not just the Catholic church but all those men and women of different denominations and different faiths whose judgment I respect. The people to whom I pay the closest attention are those who are clearly men and women both of prayer and of justice. I would walk a long way and listen with great care to prophetic figures like Helder Camara, or South Africa's Archbishop Desmond Tutu. These and many in our own country are the disciples whom God has put to the test, tried in the furnace of suffering and humiliation. I believe we ignore them at our peril.

But it is not just the churchpeople who have a monopoly on the word of God. There are other men and women, often unbelievers, who speak with authority about truth and justice. We must be alert, poised like Elijah at the mouth of his cave to catch the Word, and not be fooled into disregarding it because it comes from the mouth of someone whose religion, political stance, or cultural background is alien to our own.

We must listen also to the signs of the times, to the voice of the poor, to revolutions, to the movements of social change in our society. We are in and of this world and we will only discover its truthful core and tender heart if we are open and loving to it.

Those of us who are carers must listen in particular to the "little ones" who have been given to us to cherish. Children, the handicapped, the sick and the dying often have a directness and simplicity which gives them an access to the truth which is denied to the more complex of us; we do well to attend to our "clients" for it is out of the mouths of babes and sucklings that the most devastating of truths sometimes come.

And lastly, of course, we must listen to the word of God in our hearts. Prayer is a two-way process, a communication with the unseen God in which we not only speak but are "spoken" to in ways which are at once simple and utterly mysterious. I would like to reflect upon a particular way of listening, that which is known as making a "retreat."

The word retreat often elicits a considerable amount of respect in those who have never done it; they are surprised and rather moved that someone should go off on their own to pray. They imagine too that it will be a cozy experience, a merciful respite from the hurly-burly of the "real world," a rest, from which one will come back renewed and invigorated. In my experience however spiritual retreats are very different from that which my friends and workmates imagine. I see a retreat as a pilgrimage up the mountain, a trek into the desert, a rather daring and therefore frightening challenge to the living God to come half-way to meet me. It is, for me, a standing naked on the mountain top, a deliberate exposure to the word of God so that I may hear what God has to say to me. It is the way that I personally cash out my need and longing to be "obedient," to cleave to the will of the Father.

There are a number of different ways in which one can go "on retreat." I would not like to say that one way is better than another; it is a matter of what is available when you are free and what suits you best. Many people find that a "preached" retreat suits their needs. They go to a monastery or retreat center and, with a group of like-minded people, listen two or three times a day to a preacher who will talk upon a particular theme. In between talks they will walk, read, discuss, or pray according to their inclination and needs. Such retreats may last three days or as long as a week and can be a source of much spiritual nourishment.

Another way is to go for a time to a monastic house and join as closely as possible in the liturgy and way of life of the community. Many monasteries have guest houses and some of them welcome retreatants into choir with the monks or nuns. Other communities prefer to protect their "space" and keep retreatants at arm's length, allowing them to be present at the liturgy but not to join in it. There is much joy and support to be gained from such monastic visits, for most outsiders find the sung office both beautiful and uplifting and it is so spaced as to happily fill an otherwise long day. There is, of course, usually the possibility of a few conversations with one of the monks or sisters so that the retreatant will receive advice about matters of the spirit. I have a deep love of the monastic liturgy and find exposure to the mystery of the monastic life always leaves me with the heightened sense of awe at the God who calls young men and women to make an apparent holocaust of their lives.

Another, rather harder way of seeking God is with the Jesuits. I say harder because the retreats are normally conducted in silence with extended daily periods of prayer and one-to-one "spiritual direction." The first time I made an Ignatian retreat I was in Chile, and was trying to work out whether God was calling me to be a nun. I left my home for a week and went to stay in an almost deserted retreat house on the outskirts of the city. The priest who was directing me came each day and we talked for an hour or so. The rest of the time I spoke to no one. I prayed about five hours a day, walked in the garden and read my Bible. That is all. I found the experience staggering. Never before had anyone taken my relationship with God so seriously and the priest's manner made me equally determined to listen.

I have made many similar retreats in the last few years, although rarely for more than a few days. Each time I find the experience quite hard because, after a very active life, three days of complete withdrawal from stimuli can be unsettling. I do not always sleep very well and sometimes I get very low. Why then do I do it? Sometimes I too ask myself, Why?! The answer is, of course, that in some way that I cannot quite identify, these retreats are the occasion of an encounter with God. Sometimes these encounters have been extremely painful for I have been forced to rethink areas of my life that I thought were settled. Mostly though, these days, my experience is of long periods of weariness and aridity, which are nevertheless satisfactory. The Lord is somehow present, even in the insomnia and the depression. There are too the moments of rare joy when one's heart swells, and in the deep stillness that follows one is quite sure that the Lord was in this place: "He wears the ungathered blossom of quiet; stiller he than a deep well at noon, or lovers met; than sleep or the heart after wrath. He is the silence following great words of peace" (Rupert Brooke).

These periods of formal retreat have become a regular part of my life and I would see them as integral to my particular style of discipleship. I am, of course, not alone in this for an increasing number of men and women involved in apostolic work take time out for deliberate "listening" and discernment. This retreat from the "marketplace" to the desert is for busy people an act of faith and of humility. It is a gesture which says I believe in God. I believe so deeply that I will leave the work to which I have given my life and go to a place apart and do nothing. I will write no letters, read no books, take no telephone calls. I will, for a time, let go the strings with which I manipulate my life and be still before God. This is not a holiday nor a few days rest, but a maneuver which is deadly serious. I will lay down my load, clear my mind and say, "Speak, Lord, for your servant is listening."

And speak he does. Provided we really clear space in our lives and hearts, the Lord will speak. Not in so many words, of course, but through intuition, ideas, and movements of the heart, expressed in our feelings, in our experience of love or distaste, anguish or conflict. The Lord makes himself known as he did to Elijah in the story in 1 Kings 19.

Elijah was on the run from Jezebel who was out to get him and he traveled far into the desert to hide. Exhausted, he sat down under a furze tree, and, wishing he were dead, said, "Lord, I've had enough. Take my life, I'm no better than my ancestors." The Lord responded with that marvelous practicality of the divinity and sent him, not a sermon or an absolution but a tray of hot scones and a flask of coffee (well, water, really).

"Get up and eat," he was told, "or the journey will be too long for you."

So he got up and ate and drank and went on for forty days and forty nights until he reached Horeb, the mountain of God. When he had arrived at his destination Elijah sat down in the cave to await the word of the Lord. Then he was told, "Go out and stand on the mountain before Yahweh." Then came the pyrotechnics, the storms, the wind, the earthquake, and then a fire. But, surprise, surprise, the Lord was not in any of these. Then at last there came a gentle breeze and Elijah covered his face, for he recognized the voice of God.

The Elijah story makes clear that the Lord's voice is often so quiet that we must stand very still if we are to hear it. True, there may be the burning bush or the Damascus road experiences, but these are usually once in a lifetime encounters, experiences of call or correction that leave us in no doubt that we have been touched by God. For the rest of the time, if we are to listen seriously we must go a little way into the desert, turn off our transistor and listen.

And how to interpret these movements of the spirit? May we not read the message incorrectly, get carried away by religious fervor or emotion and make a crazy decision that we will come to regret later?

It is indeed possible to get things out of perspective or make unwise decisions when the heart is troubled; for this reason most people who feel called to a life of radical discipleship do well to seek advice from someone skilled in spiritual direction. Just as the handicapped, the troubled or the dying need someone to accompany them on their journey, so too do we need a skilled friend as we make our way toward God.

The practice of spiritual direction is an old one in the church and indeed in many of the Eastern religions. The disciple seeks out a *guru* or wise father and opens his heart to him, asking for correction, for help, and for guidance. For some people all that is needed is a little advice in prayer from a person more experienced than themselves. Others, however, whose lives are more complex and decision-making therefore more difficult, need a director with special skills to help them discern what the Lord is asking. The Jesuits, in particular, and those sisters whose spirituality is based upon the teachings of St. Ignatius, have made a special study of the art of spiritual direction. These men and women receive training in psychology and counseling skills as well as in strictly spiritual matters, for the workings of the mind and spirit are inexorably intertwined. If we are to understand the causes of conflict in grown men and women, we must have knowledge not just of the manner in which childhood events can influence, or changes in mood alter, the response to a given stimulus. Modern Ignatian spiritual direction is founded not just upon a life of prayer and knowledge of the scriptures, but upon an understanding of the way men and women function. With such a guide we may embark upon a process of *discernment*, working to clarify what the spirit is saying in our hearts.

This word *discernment* is a key one in Ignatian spirituality. In his Principle of Foundation, Ignatius writes:

> Man is created to love, serve and praise God our Lord and by this means save his soul. All other things in the world are created for man to help him in the end for which he was created. From this it follows that we must use things so far as they help us attain this end and we must discard things in so far as they hinder us.

If we believe that each of us is called by name to serve God in a special way and that each calling is individual, then it follows that we must discover, *discern*, what God is asking, not of Christians in general, but of *us* in particular. This seems to me to be fundamental to the spiritual life; we need to know what God is asking not of the Pope or of the Carmelite sister down the road, but of *us*, whether we be housewife, film star, nurse, or medical director of a hospice for the dying.

Hilda of Whitby, a seventh-century nun who was the head of a double monastery (for men and women) and a spiritual adviser to kings and bishops, has a marvelous way of putting this call to individual service:

> Trade with the gifts that God has given you. Bend your minds to holy learning that you may escape the fretting moth of littleness of mind which would wear out your souls. Brace your wills to action that they may not be the spoil of weak desires. Raise your heart and lips in song which gives courage to the soul. Being buffeted by trials, learn to laugh; being rebuked, give thanks; and having failed, determine to succeed.

If we take Ignatius's statement that we are created to serve God, and Hilda's advice to trade with the gifts that God has given us, we have two elements essential to discernment; as in the gospel story of the talents we are each given an individual gift with which to serve and we must work that gift, not bury it in the ground. Discernment is about the *interaction* between the Spirit of God moving in our hearts and the way we respond to that Spirit, the way we live our lives. It is about a way of living with the ears always open to the Spirit, with the eyes like those of the servant girl in the psalm, always upon the hand of her mistress. Discernment is about obedience, about living one's life abandoned to God; it is, in essence, about freedom.

There are two main aspects of living discernment. The first is in major decision-making processes, life-changing events where one is choosing a state of life or a career. The second is a more subtle, ongoing affair, a way of living day by day, minute by minute in an ever-increasing condition of sensitivity, of openness to the Spirit of God. Let us look first at a major discernment experience for it is here that we may understand it more clearly.

Let us say, for example, that a man or woman gets an offer of a different job. They find the offer exciting, interesting, and must decide whether or not to accept it. It is not just a question of promotion, of prestige, of money. The new post may be more responsible, more important, better paid, but that in itself is not enough. The person must decide: Is this the best way *for me* to be using my gifts? Is this the best way I can serve God? What will happen to the people I now serve if I leave them? Can I be replaced? Will the new post bring me new ways of serving, expand my caring, bring me closer to God and God's people? Or will it perhaps distance me from the people I am most gifted for? There are too the more human elements: Will this job stretch me beyond my capacity so that I will be at risk of losing the more gentle, creative side of my nature? Will it distance me too far from the people who support me, from those I need and who need me? And what of my friends and family, of those I have been given to take care of? If I am married, will my spouse and children be happy and fulfilled in a new place, or will my gain be their loss?

There are so many things to be worked out in any major decision and if we wish to do it wisely, then it is good to pray, reflect and discuss with an impartial adviser. It is a question of balance, of reflection and of logical thinking done in the light of prayer. It is a question too of listening to the heart. How do *I feel* when I think about this proposed change? Do I feel calm, peaceful, and right about it, or do I feel at some level disturbed, nagged by doubts? Discernment in its essence is not just about prayer, about asking God for guidance, but about listening to the inner voice of conscience, and of emotion, of the heart.

This listening, learned in the more formal situation of retreat, may be carried out into daily life. Once I have become familiar with my inner voices I can recognize them more easily. As I drive my car or sit at home in the evening I can reflect gently upon the events of the day. Some things I did or said may leave me with that deep peaceful sense of having acted from my true center. Others, however, leave a feeling of discord. That which, at the time I said it, seemed witty or clever, I may now realize was wounding and would have been better not said. Little by little, in this way we can learn from experience and perhaps become more gentle, more compassionate people. It is a balance between learning to accept our weakness of temperament and working to become more of that which we are called to be. It is what the Benedictines call *Conversio Morem*: a change in manners. This is their only vow: to respond to the voice of the Spirit calling them to grow in the likeness of Christ. There seems no reason why it should not be ours.

⊰{ 18 }⊱

EMPTY OUT YOUR TEACUP GOD

The Tao that can be told is not the eternal Tao
The name that can be named is not the eternal name.

Lao Tsu
from *Tao Te Ching*

This last chapter is by way of being a "credo." It is an account of the God whom I meet in my life of "sharing the darkness" and of how I personally have made sense of the world in which I live.

The Indian Jesuit psychologist Tony de Mello is quoted as saying, "Empty out your teacup God"—a marvelous, withering and twentieth-century way of telling us that our God is too small. A few years ago I would have thought that a professional carer's God-concept was his or her own private business; but the longer I work in the field of caring, the more important it seems that we do not get hung up on false gods, however comforting. It matters for three reasons. Firstly, as I have tried to show, we will damage those we care for if we are purveyors of a theology in which illness is seen as a punishment for sins or physical healing is declared freely available to those with sufficient faith.

Secondly, we ourselves will come unstuck if we search for facile explanations of the mystery of suffering instead of bowing down in baffled awe before the one, holy, unknowable God.

Thirdly, as adult human beings, we have no business clinging to childhood beliefs when we should be letting go in faith to follow the truth. Our hearts are for filling, our minds are for blowing, and our idols for shattering into a thousand pieces. In her book *Holy the Firm*, Annie Dillard struggles to wrest a meaning from the tragic accident of a young girl burnt in a plane crash:

> Today is Friday, November 20th. Julie Norwich is in the hospital, burned; we can get no word of her condition. People released from burn wards, I once read, have a very high suicide rate. They had not realized, before they were burnt, that life could include suffering or that they personally could be permitted such pain . . .

In Chapter 9, I quoted Annie Dillard's reaction to the story of Christ's encounter with the man born blind. The disciples, ever curious, asked Jesus why the man should have been thus afflicted. Was it, they said, his fault or his parents'? Jesus' reply, "meager, baffling, and infuriating," was that "the works of God should be made manifest." Dillard reacts in a fury:

> The works of God made manifest? Do we really need more victims to remind us that we're all victims? Is this some sort of a parade for which a conquering army shines up its terrible guns and rolls them up and down the street for the people to see? Do we need blind men stumbling about, and little flame-faced children, to remind us what God can — and will — do?

I find this angry questioning marvelous for it throws piety and pussyfooting to the wind and asks the questions we all long to ask. Why did God permit the earthquake in Guatemala or Mexico? Why must Derek die of cancer, when he is so young, so good, so loved by his wife and children? And what of the thirty-two-year-old girl whose body I saw last time I went to the undertakers — flown in from Germany where she'd taken her own life in a fit of depression? Why, why? Oh God, why? What the hell is going on here?

> Again rises from the heart of suffering the ancient
> cry,

O God, why? O God, how long?
And the cry is met with silence.

Jim Cotter
from *Healing More or Less*

I like, too, Annie Dillard's answers, though I do not claim that they are true. How can I know, how can she? All I know is that they satisfy some of my intellectual yearnings for answers to impossible questions.

Do we need . . . little flame-faced children to remind us what God can — and will — do? Yes, in fact, we do. We do need reminding, not of what God can do, but of what he cannot do, or will not, which is to catch time in its free fall and stick a nickel's worth of sense into our days. And we need reminding of what time can do, must only do; churn out enormity at random, and beat it, with God's blessing, into our heads: that we are *created,* sojourners in a land we did not make, a land with no meaning of itself and no meaning we can make for it alone. Who are we to demand explanations of God? (And what monsters of perfection would we be if we did not?) We forget ourselves, picnicking; we forget where we are. There is no such thing as a freak accident. "God is at home," says Meister Eckhart. "We are in the far country." (*Holy the Firm*)

I find this concept of forgetting ourselves picnicking very powerful. When we are well and successful we do indeed lose sight of who and where we are. We build our hospitals, play with our computers, travel to the moon in rockets, and fancy ourselves as lords of the earth. And then, if we are lucky, we have the mat pulled out from under our feet by an earthquake, a tornado, or by illness and we rediscover ourselves as creatures.

Dillard's language is not easy to understand, but perhaps it is hardly surprising for she is struggling to talk about the unknowable God, the God that we are always trying to tame, to tie down, and to manipulate to do what we want. Sometimes it is difficult to realize that we are talking about the same God. Is this God of the mystics' "dazzling dark," the same Jesus whom we beg to heal our wounds, the same God that I invoke to start my recalcitrant car on a cold morning? Of course it is, for there is only one God. It is *we* who need to understand God this way and that, to call him Jesus, Lord, Abba, Father, El Shaddai, Yahweh. Christians, Hindus, Jews, Muslims, Sikhs and so on: we each have our different needs—to light candles, to strew flowers, to offer sweetmeats. And that is O.K., for that is the way God made us. All God asks is that we worship as best we can and that we do not delude ourselves into thinking that we can contain or manipulate God. Having emptied out our teacup God, we find him everywhere and meet him face to face in the scriptures of those we used to think of as heathen:

> There is no God but He, the
> Living, the Everlasting.
> Slumber seizes Him not, neither sleep;
> to Him belongs all that is in the heavens and in the
>   earth.
> Who is there that shall intercede with Him
> save by His leave?
> He knows what lies before them
> and what is after them,
> and they comprehend not anything of His
> knowledge save such as He wills.
> His throne comprises the heavens and the earth;
> the preserving of them oppresses Him not.
> He is the All-high, the All-glorious.
>
> *The Koran*, Sura 2.255

But although we "comprehend not anything of His" we are born to try. It is in our nature to struggle to understand the ways of God, to argue with him like Job, until we are reduced again to silence. Each of us, therefore, must follow our own lines of questioning, searching, piecing together the evidence, striving to penetrate the mystery. It so happens that I find myself most at home with the writings of the mystics. Others may not find them helpful. Like Annie Dillard, I am drawn to Meister Eckhart's vision of the God who strips us of our support system so that we may be freed for him. To others this kind of God-talk is unacceptable. But before we dismiss each other's theology we must remember that we are all searching, playing with ideas, struggling with the unseen God. The following passage from Eckhart makes more sense to me than anything else I have read about suffering:

> The faithful God often lets his friends fall sick and lets every prop on which they lean be knocked out from under them. It is a great joy to loving people to be able to do important things such as watching, fasting, and the like, besides sundry more difficult undertakings. In such things they find their joy, and their stay and hope. Thus their pious works are supports, stays, or footings to them. Our Lord wants to take these things all away, for he would like to be their only stay. He does this because of his simple goodness and mercy. He wants nothing more than his own goodness. He will not be influenced in the least to give or do by any act of ours. Our Lord wants his friends to be rid of such notions. That is why he removes every prop, so that he alone may support them. It is his will to give greatly, but only because of his own free goodness, so that he shall be their support and they, finding themselves to be nothing at all, may know how great the generosity of God is. For the more helpless and destitute the mind that turns to God for support can be, the deepest the person penetrates God and the more sensitive he is to God's most valuable gifts. Man must build on God alone. (*Talks of Instruction*, no. 10)

Eckhart clearly believes in a God who permits suffering rather on the Job model. At first sight this seems an outrageous idea. How can we believe in a loving God who allows good people to get cancer or other unpleasant diseases? And yet, if we think it through, how can we *not* believe it? Good people clearly do suffer persecution, accidents and illness. So what is going on? It seems to me there are four possibilities. The first is that we are all deluding ourselves and that there is no God at all: things just happen in a random sort of way. The second possibility is that God is not able to control the forces of nature or evil and is powerless to stop things happening. That way God could be like us: good and loving but powerless to stop the avalanche or the tornado. The third is that God is quite capable of preventing something happening but does not choose to intervene. God sees the dictator take power, the political prisoners arrested and tortured, but does not move to stay the executioner's hand. The Jesuit poet Dan Berrigan captures the anguished cry of those who see evil triumph, their prayers for deliverance apparently ignored:

> I see the wicked glide by
> sleek in their velvet hearses
> rich beyond measure, egos
> puffed like adders.

> No sons of misfortune these:
> no cares shadow the perfumed brows;
> a whirling of furies
> their axle tree cuts;
> the innocent die.

> I sweat like a beast
> for the fate of my people.
> Is God
> ignorant, blank eyed,
> deaf, far distant,
> bought off, grown old? . . .

> Why then endure
> why thirst for justice?
> Your kingdom-come
> a mirage, never comes.

> I sweat like a beast
> my nightmare is life long
> And where in the world
> are you?
>
> Daniel Berrigan
> "Psalm 73," *Uncommon Prayer*

The fourth possibility is that God is somehow *involved* in every person's life and actually *arranges* that some people suffer more than others because it is part of the great cosmic plan.

I cannot say I find any one of these four options easily acceptable but I would tend toward the fourth: a belief in a God who both permits suffering and is somehow deeply involved in his creation and his creatures, although we are at a loss to understand his ways. My own experience of personal suffering and many years of working for the oppressed and the dying has left me knowing less but believing more. This is my "credo":

I believe that God
has the whole world
in his hands.

He is not a bystander
at the pain of the world.
He does not stand
like Peter,
wringing his hands
in the shadows,
but is there,
in the dock,
on the rack,
high on the gallows tree.

He is *in* the pain
of the lunatic,
the tortured,
those wracked by grief.
His is the blood
that flows in the gutter.
His are the veins burned by heroin,
his the lungs choked by AIDS.
His is the heart
broken by suffering,
his the despair
of the mute,

the oppressed,
the man with the gun to his head.

He is the God of Paradox.

In this piece of spaced-out prose (I do not pretend that it is poetry!) I have tried to capture two of the most mysterious elements of our Christian faith: that God is the all-powerful creator of this world and at the same time God suffers impotently at the heart of it. And as if that was not hard enough to take on board, we believe that this same God who allows/permits/connives at/causes suffering, is all-loving and all-caring. He is the God who told us not to worry because we are "worth more than many sparrows" and yet sits silently by while children starve to death and pregnant women are raped and bayoneted to death. Well may the poet cry, "And where in the world are you?" (Berrigan).

I would like to leave the "why me" question there, for I have no answer to it. Let it remain like a friendly punchbag hanging in the corner of the screaming room, upon which we can vent our rage and sadness, our questions and our impotence. Let us turn now to an equally mysterious and fascinating aspect of Christian doctrine, the concept of redemptive suffering.

This doctrine is very important to me personally—I believe it passionately and it sustains me in my daily contact with the dying and in my consciousness of the hungry and the oppressed. Once again, however, it plunges me into the mystery of the God of paradox for I must hold in some sort of creative tension two apparently contradictory beliefs: that I am called to continue Christ's ministry of healing, to pour myself out for the hungry and the desolate, the sick, and the oppressed, *and* that all this unmerited suffering which I am struggling to prevent and alleviate is redeeming the world.

Mercifully, as it happens, I *don't* have any problems reconciling these two beliefs for I have long since learned to be comfortable with mystery. Perhaps it is just the type of person I am, or perhaps it is that I find the two ideas so abundantly clear that I do not find it necessary to worry about it. It is, however, a quantum leap from the idea that *Jesus* by suffering redeemed the world to the notion that *all* unwanted suffering is redemptive, so I will try to explain how I arrived at this conviction. As Christians, we are familiar with the idea that Christ died for our sins, and for some people the details of the death of the historical Jesus are integral to their devotion. As a Catholic child I was brought up to meditate upon the Stations of the Cross — the milestones of Jesus' journey from Pilate's court to Calvary, but I no longer find this type of devotion helpful. Perhaps my enforced familiarity with the suffering of men and women of our own time has made the dwelling upon the reenactment of the crucifixion seem stylized and sentimental. I find it hard to weep about the crowning of thorns when I think about modern-day torture centers in Latin America. Frankly, I find myself unable to meditate upon either — it sickens me. Of much greater interest to me than the details of Jesus' torture and death is the theology *behind* it. For that we need to turn to Isaiah, to what is known as the "Song of the Servant."

The "Suffering Servant of Yahweh" is a mysterious figure in Isaiah, "a man of suffering and acquainted with grief," who somehow, *by his suffering*, takes upon himself the sins of the people. The Servant is, moreover, a man singled out for this task. It is not that ill fortune has overcome him by chance, but rather that he has been chosen for this task from the womb. In Isaiah 42, in the first of the four songs, the prophet declares that Yahweh called him by name before he was born, singled him out to serve in the cause of right. He was molded and formed for his task and then appointed as a leader, given his mandate to open the eyes of the blind, to free captives from prison and those who live in the darkness from the dungeon.

That Jesus identified himself with the prophet is clear, for he used a parallel text from Isaiah when he began his preaching ministry in the temple making his own the call to bring good news to the poor, freedom to captives, and sight to the blind. It is however quite uncanny the way the events preceding the crucifixion are mirrored in the Song of the Servant:

> For my part, I made no resistance,
> neither did I turn away.
> I offered my back to those who struck me,

my cheeks to those who tore at my beard;
I did not cover my face
against insult and spittle.

Isa. 50:5-6

It is in the fourth song, however, that the concept of redemptive
suffering is spelled out:

As the crowds were appalled on seeing him
—so disfigured did he look
that he seemed no longer human—
so will the crowds be astonished at him,
and kings stand speechless before him;
for they shall see something never told
and witness something never heard before:
"Who could believe what we have heard,
and to whom has the power of Yahweh been
    revealed?"
Like a sapling he grew up in front of us,
like a root in arid ground.
Without beauty, without majesty (we saw him),
no looks to attract our eyes;
a thing despised and rejected by men,
a man of sorrows and familiar with suffering,
a man to make people screen their faces;
he was despised and we took no account of him.

And yet ours were the sufferings he bore,
ours the sorrows he carried.
But we, we thought of him as someone punished,
struck by God, and brought low.
Yet he was pierced through for our faults,
crushed for our sins.
On him lies a punishment that brings us peace,
and through his wounds we are healed.

Isa. 52:14-53:5

This passage came alive for me in a singularly poignant way
a few weeks ago when I read from it to comfort a man who was

sobbing in despair at the uselessness of his suffering. He had a cancer in his mouth which had destroyed his tongue so that he could barely speak and it was now invading his face. At that moment he was for me the man so disfigured he was no longer human, the man to make people screen their faces.

I first became interested in the Song of the Servant and its message when I was at Ampleforth Abbey, living as a sort of monk manqué, attending the Divine Office and dabbling a little in scripture and theology. I was struck particularly by the terrifying description of the man of sorrows, a creature disfigured, without beauty, "a man to make people screen their faces." This image, so familiar, made me think not of Jesus and his crucifixion but of the people of South America and in particular of the people that I left behind in the torture centers and the concentration camps in Chile. Not that I personally saw people who had been mutilated—the authorities were too careful for that. Those who had been badly hurt were isolated until their wounds healed or sometimes they just disappeared. But I knew from my own experience of torture and from the accounts of my companions that the brutalized are not a pretty sight. Could it be, I wondered, that these people, too, the men hung naked and upside down on the "pau de arara" or the women raped and violated by dogs were somehow atoning for the sins of their captors?

At first it seems preposterous to think of Chilean Marxists bearing the sins of the CIA upon their bruised and bloodstained shoulders. But why not? Is not the "parilla" the twentieth-century equivalent of the cross, the throwing of a man bound with barbed wire to his death from a helicopter, the counterpart of crucifixion? The more I thought about it, the more convinced I became that if Jesus' suffering was redemptive, so too was the suffering of those who had laid down their lives for their friends.

If this seems an absurd bending of the scriptures to political ends, let me hasten to quote St. Paul in my defense: "It makes me happy to suffer for you, as I am suffering now, and in my body to do what I can to make up all that has still to be undergone by Christ for the sake of his body, the Church" (Col. 1:24). Perhaps then we can see Christ's redemptive act as an ongoing drama in which we are all players. The question which I ask myself as I write is this: can we see *all* unmerited suffering as redemptive? Or is its redemptive power contingent upon the sufferer's mental attitude? One thinks of examples of the heroic fortitude of people like Thérèse of Lisieux, offering her suffering from terminal tuberculosis to God. Much nearer home, I recall a young Catholic woman dying of cancer who asked me one day, "How can I *use* suffering for others?" It is hard to imagine that such an offering is rejected; the pain of these women must somehow be taken up like a holocaust and used we know not how.

Moving just a step laterally from these people who *offer* their pain for others, I think of all the good Christian people whose theology does not encompass this kind of prayer or language. They suffer bravely, loving and giving to the end. What happens to *their* gifts? Surely it must go, albeit unlabeled, to the same heavenly sorting office? But what of the atheist? I think in particular of Margaret, a woman I mentioned earlier on. An unbeliever, she radiated the sort of serenity and generosity one expects of saints and died a magnificent selfless death, her life poured out daily for what?

From there, of course, we move naturally to those men and women who somehow never receive the grace to accept their suffering and die a sad inward-looking and frankly selfish death. We see these people at the hospice from time to time: men and women whose horizons are shrunk by suffering and who will call out to have their pillows straightened when they can see the nurses attending to someone in pain, right in the next bed. These are the poorest of my people, and it is hard to love them. Is their suffering worthless in the divine strategy? I doubt it. How can it be, for people's psychological and emotional well-being is not a clear-cut issue of heroism and sin. We all have different gifts and different weaknesses. Some are conditioned by a loveless childhood to fight their own corner and cannot take on board the needs of others.

Lastly, of course, there are those who, in purely human terms, get what is coming to them. What price the murderer's agony as he awaits execution or the pain of the child molester as he is beaten, cringing, to a pulp by the other prisoners? Or the terrorist felled by the bullets of police or rival factions? They surely

must fall unnoticed into the pit whence they came. But do they?
I doubt it.

If I can forgive my torturers, if Gordon Wilson can forgive
the terrorists who killed his daughter, what much greater loving
space must we imagine in the heart of our all-seeing, all-loving
God. The lines that follow are a continuation of my own particular "credo," the beliefs that have crystallized during the past
few years, when exposure to suffering has become an everyday
experience, a part of life:

I believe,
no pain is lost.
No tear unmarked,
no cry of anguish
dies unheard,
lost in the hail of gunfire
or blanked out by the padded cell.
I believe that pain
and prayer
are somehow saved,
processed,
stored,
used in the Divine Economy.
The blood
shed in Salvador
will irrigate the heart
of some financier
a million miles away.
The terror,
pain,
despair,
swamped
by lava, flood or earthquake
will be caught up
like mist and fall again,
a gentle rain
on arid hearts
or souls despairing

in the back streets
of Brooklyn.

No doubt when I talk like this, *my* God is too small. Of course
he is. How can we know what God is about—or even if there is
a God? We can only struggle with the facts as we see them,
ponder them deep in our hearts and extrapolate from our own
experience. And when we have done that, we can only say, "This
is what makes sense to me. This is how I think it works." The
great joke, of course, is that the more we believe, the less we
know. I cannot put it better than Fyn's Anna:

> When you're little you "understand" Mister God. He sits
> up there on his throne, a golden one of course; he has
> whiskers and crown and everyone is singing hymns like
> mad to him. God is useful and usable. You can ask him
> for things, he can strike your enemies deader than a door-
> nail and he is pretty good at putting hexes on the bully
> next door, like warts and things. Mister God is so "under-
> standable," so useful and so usable, he is like some object,
> perhaps the most important object of all, but nevertheless
> an object, and absolutely understandable. Later on you
> "understand" him to be a bit different but you are still
> able to grasp what he is. Even though you "understand"
> him, he doesn't seem to understand you! He doesn't seem
> to understand that you simply must have a new bike, but
> your "understanding" of him changes a bit more. In what-
> ever way or state you understand Mister God, so you
> diminish his size. He becomes an understandable entity
> among other understandable entities. So Mister God keeps
> on shedding bits all the way through your life until the
> time comes you admit freely and honestly that you don't
> understand Mister God at all. At this point you have let
> Mister God be his proper size and wham, there he is laugh-
> ing at you. (*Mr. God, This Is Anna*)

Perhaps Anna, the down-to-earth child who walked and
talked with Mr. God and died a messy death impaled upon a
fence post, is a model for us all. We too must be Easter people,

deeply rooted in the world and its pain but holding always within the same focus the God who made us and who alone makes sense of our living and our dying.

At first this seems a tall order, but we forget: Easter people grow up to become the children of Pentecost. Right at the heart of the mystery of suffering is the grace that sustains us all, carers and cared for alike. It comes as freely and as surely as the sunrise, piercing the blackness of grief and despair, restoring once again the hope of things unseen.